The Complete Photo Guide to

ART QUILTING

Creative Publishing
international

First published in the United States of America by
Creative Publishing international, Inc., a member of
Quarto Publishing Group USA Inc.
400 First Avenue North
Suite 400
Minneapolis, MN 55401
1-800-328-3895
www.creativepub.com or www.Qbookshop.com

Visit www.Craftside.Typepad.com for a behind-the-scenes
peek at our crafty world!

ISBN: 978-1-58923-689-9

Printed in China
10 9 8 7

Library of Congress Cataloging-in-Publication Data

Stein, Susan, 1945-
  The complete photo guide to art quilting / Susan Stein.
      p. cm. – (Complete photo guide)
   ISBN 978-1-58923-689-9 (pbk.)
   1. Quilting–Technique. 2. Art quilts. I. Title.

TT835 .S7195
746.46–dc23

2011043569

Photography Coordinator: Joanne Wawra
Copy Editor: Catherine Broberg
Proofreader: Karen Ruth
Book and Cover Design: Kim Winscher
Page Layout: Laurie Young
Photography: Kit Eastman: 21 (top), 99 (left);
Maria Elkins: 110, 111; Elizabeth Palmer-Spilker: 196, 197;
Rhea Pappas: 145, 169-179; Sharon Vitt: 3, 180, 181;
Petronella J Ytsma: 43 (bottom)

The Complete Photo Guide to
ART QUILTING

Creative Publishing
international

CONTENTS

What is an Art Quilt?

There are simple answers to this question, like "it's a non-traditional quilt," but the term art quilt means many things and everyone will have a different opinion. Generally, art quilts are made for display only and not for beds. Art quilts vary in size from tiny 4" (10 cm) square pieces to huge pieces made for corporate walls. Yet they don't even have to lie flat against the wall—in fact, some are mounted on a series of sticks and stand on the floor while others are suspended from the ceiling on clear monofilament.

Since art quilts do not have to withstand daily use and handling, they can be constructed in different ways and contain different materials from traditional quilts made for regular use. Good construction is still valued and the principles of design and composition come into play much more, since the quilt will be viewed hanging on a wall like the piece of art it is. Hanging mechanisms are built into an art quilt, are designed to support the quilt for long periods of time, and are often hidden from view. In some situations, quilts made for public buildings are required to be fireproof or are hung behind Plexiglas. Indeed, art quilts made for public spaces often carry with them very specific requests, like being easily removable or firmly attached to the wall to prevent theft.

Art quilts often comply with the rules of traditional quilting in that they have three layers and stitching to hold the layers together. However, they break the rules in many cases and exhibits of art quilts carefully spell out the new rules in their entry forms. Art quilters who want to exhibit should expect to follow stringent requirements for photography and electronic submissions, making the quilt's creation just a part of the whole process.

Surface design has become a major component of most pieces. Some artists dye or paint their own fabric, while others purchase fabric from the many artists selling one-of-a-kind cloth. Art cloth is yet another offshoot of art quilting and lengths of fabric with no stitching or layers at all make up whole exhibits of their own. Some fabric isn't fabric at all but spun polyester, Tyvek, handmade paper, wool or silk roving, metal, etc. Even foil candy wrappers find their way into contemporary quilts!

Art quilts may be comprised of rows of blocks like traditional quilts, but more often they cover the surface with a less formal arrangement of elements. Some quilts are just one piece of fabric with painting or dyeing plus lots of stitching to add detail. Quilts may be divided into separate units meant to hang together in close proximity. Both hand and machine techniques are used extensively in making art quilts, and piecing and appliqué both play important parts in construction. Appliqué in all its many forms is probably the most common technique used because it allows for great freedom.

An art quilter may approach the design process in a variety of ways. Some people use a sketchbook to plan projects or record ideas on the run, while others make complex diagrams on graph paper. Some use computer design programs to map out a plan. Others take some fabric out of their stash, hang it on the design wall, and let ideas percolate throughout the course of the day's activities, adding coordinating fabrics and trims to the wall as they appear while digging through the stash for other things. Some quilts begin with photo manipulation and printing, using the computer and printer to transfer images to cloth. In the case of commissions, the customer's requirements may dictate the design of the project.

The Complete Photo Guide to Art Quilting will take you from the kernel of an idea through all the stages of making an art quilt. There will be lots of inspiration along the way and some projects for getting a jump start. The most important part of becoming a good art quilter is to practice being an art quilter! No amount of dreaming or wishing will make you good at anything you want to

accomplish—you must get into your work area and begin something, even if it goes into the wastebasket later. Set aside time, no matter how little, to work on your art as many days a week as possible. Creative time is very therapeutic and stimulates greater productivity in other areas of life, so it shouldn't be considered a waste of time. If necessary, involve other people—especially children—in their own projects alongside you to allow you time to work. Putting small studies up on the design wall can keep the juices flowing and lead to further development during the next session. Having even the smallest area

to work in that doesn't have to be cleaned up can lead to continuous progress over a period of time. Eventually, you will develop a personal style or voice in your work. It may take years of playing and experimenting, but what a fun journey! Working in a series promotes the generation of lots of "what if?" ideas and makes your style recognizable. Again, doing the work will generate results, no matter how many false starts or hesitation points there are along the way. Learning happens just as much from failures as it does from successes. Dive in!

GETTING STARTED

Most people don't just wake up one day and say, "Today I will become an art quilter." Rather, quilters gradually realize that traditional quilting can be more fun if they add their own individual flavor to a project, or they see a new way to make their own fabric and a project grows from that. Trying different techniques to decorate or embellish fabric and using different shapes and sizes from what you're accustomed to can present an interesting challenge. Creating a series of small pieces, each developing a new approach to a particular theme, is very satisfying and starts to reveal a personal style. If you are a sketchbook enthusiast, working out ideas on paper may be your approach instead of heading to the fabric stash. Working on paper also offers you a valuable resource for years to come as well as a portable way to take your work with you. As soon as you start to make original work, a design wall becomes essential and space to be creative becomes a priority. This section covers all these facets of getting started on your art quilting adventure.

Setting Up a
Work Space

It's important to have a designated work space for quilting of any kind. Putting all the supplies and equipment away after each session not only takes plenty of time, it also doesn't allow for casual evaluation of a project while doing other things. Some people set up in a large closet that they can shut the doors on; others have a whole building devoted to their passion. Organization is the key to either approach, as looking for fabrics, trims, embellishments, and threads can become a frustrating and time-consuming endeavor.

Fabric can be sorted by type, since art quilting utilizes many more materials than traditional quilting. Depending on the size of your stash, a sweater bin may suffice for each type of unusual fabric, while the cottons might go into cupboards or bookshelves. Any system you devise should protect the fabric from direct light. Most people sort their fabric by color, and you might want to mark long pieces with their measurements. If you choose to prewash your cottons, take them out of the dryer while slightly damp and fold them neatly so they are ready to head to the ironing and cutting boards when you are ready to use them.

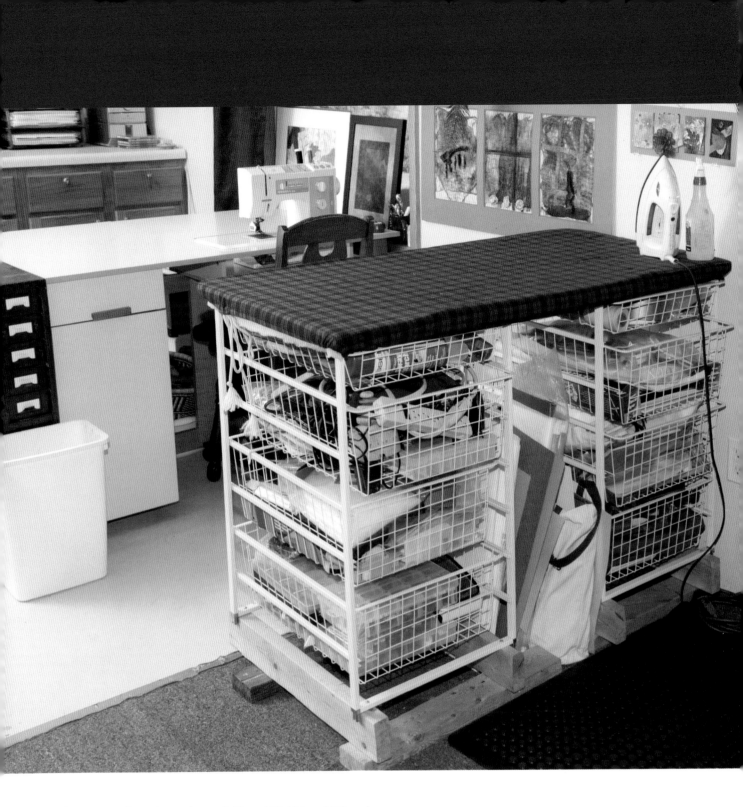

The ironing board can be a 24" x 48" (61 x 122 cm) piece of laminate covered with cotton batting and heavy fabric. A heavy cord drawstring added to the edges of the cover makes it easy to install and change when needed. Set up two towers of wire drawers as a base for the ironing board to store all the odds and ends of fusible web, interfacings, stabilizers, beads, templates, rulers, etc. Make sure the outlet for the iron is heavy duty.

(continued)

A design wall makes auditioning fabrics and designs, and evaluating work-in-progress possible. Depending on the room, a design wall can be portable or permanent. Large sheets of wall insulation foam (4' x 8' [122 x 244 cm]) are ideal because they last for years, are rigid, and are large enough to accommodate most projects. Cover the foam with cotton batting, felt, or flannel taped around the back. No pins are needed to hold small pieces of fabric onto the fuzzy surface. To install permanently, use two screws near the top to hold the sheets to the wall. For temporary installation, just lean the sheets against the wall, or cut the sheets in half and hinge them together with duct tape so they can be stashed in a closet or under the bed. For something less cumbersome, cover a large bulletin board or foam core board with batting. Create a soft design wall with batting if you need to stash it away; simply hang it from the curtains or throw it over a door. You will be amazed at how much your work improves when you can see the elements of a quilt from across the room instead of on the table surface. If the room is small, look through the back side of binoculars or snap some digital photos to get a better perspective on the design.

Adequate lighting is essential to good work conditions and good health. Portable lighting is possible if cords are safely routed to protect people and pets. If possible, set up your work area near a window as an aid in color selection and a resting place for tired eyes. Remember that every ten years, your need for light increases 10 percent, so don't ignore this part of work space set-up, and re-evaluate periodically.

(continued)

A cutting surface is needed for most projects, whether it is used for rotary cutting, cutting with a craft knife, or using a scissors. Get the largest mat your set-up can accommodate—your work and frustration level will both benefit. It can be turned over for messy work or covered with plastic. Raising the table that the cutting mat sits on will pay for itself many times over in avoiding back strain, or purchase a table especially designed for working standing up. Sections of PVC pipe or bed risers under the table legs make it possible to change the height of the table in seconds. A tiny cutting board located at the sewing machine can save time and steps—just be careful to close the safety cover on the rotary cutter every time it is used.

The kind of work you do will determine what other pieces of equipment—like computers, heat presses, sergers, and copy machines—you will need to have available. A table designated for painting can save lots of time because you can leave it set up and covered with plastic and allow things to dry while you work in another area of the studio. What is important is that you can work efficiently in an organized space that is well-lit and comfortable. Don't forget the hydraulic chair and music too.

Choosing a Format

There are no guidelines for what an art quilt should look like. It can be the size of a postcard or large enough to cover a corporate wall. It can be any shape, stretched over wooden bars, framed with glass and matting, or even projecting from the wall. Several pieces might be hung in close proximity to make a grouping. A piece might hang on the wall behind another piece that allows the viewer to see through it.

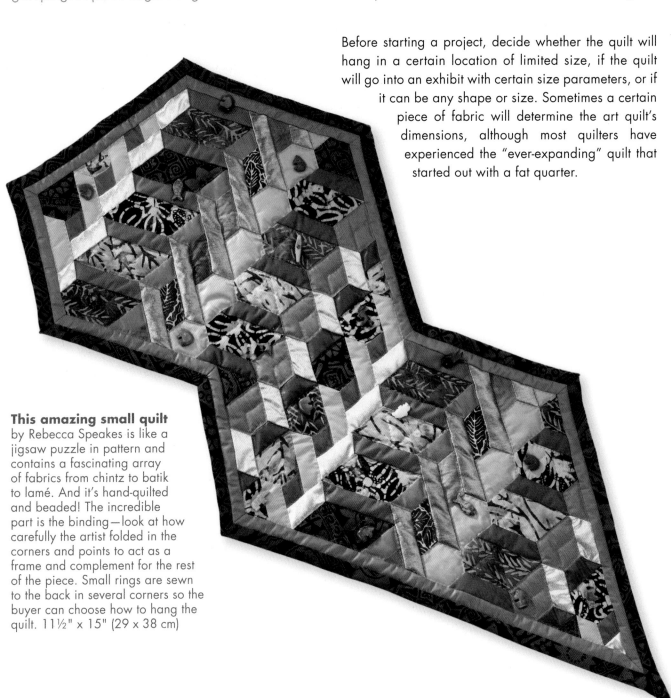

Before starting a project, decide whether the quilt will hang in a certain location of limited size, if the quilt will go into an exhibit with certain size parameters, or if it can be any shape or size. Sometimes a certain piece of fabric will determine the art quilt's dimensions, although most quilters have experienced the "ever-expanding" quilt that started out with a fat quarter.

This amazing small quilt by Rebecca Speakes is like a jigsaw puzzle in pattern and contains a fascinating array of fabrics from chintz to batik to lamé. And it's hand-quilted and beaded! The incredible part is the binding—look at how carefully the artist folded in the corners and points to act as a frame and complement for the rest of the piece. Small rings are sewn to the back in several corners so the buyer can choose how to hang the quilt. 11½" x 15" (29 x 38 cm)

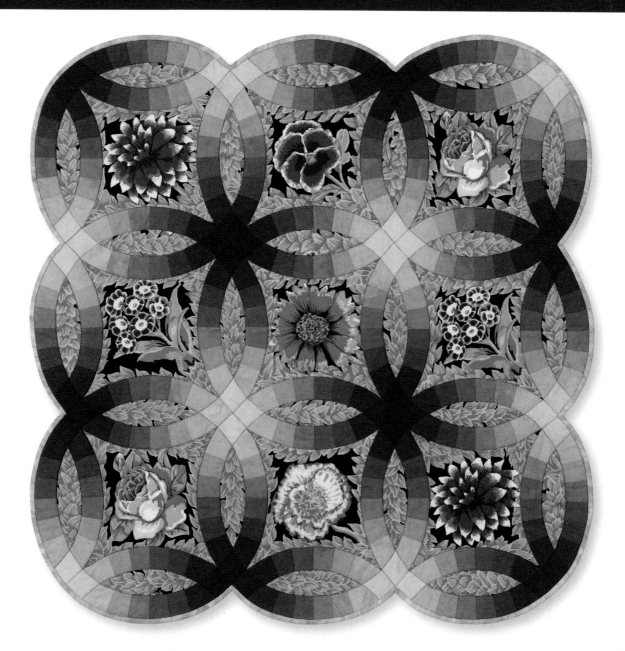

Finishing and display concerns are probably the biggest determining factors in choosing an unusual format for an art quilt. A piece with many sharp or irregular points and shapes will require very careful and time-consuming binding or a turned edge. A round or irregularly shaped piece will require special hanging sleeves and support for extended edges. Don't avoid a special shape but take it into consideration when planning. If the quilt will be entered into shows, be sure to study up on the installation guidelines and limits.

(continued)

A quilt with a curved edge
like this Double Wedding Ring calls for bias binding hand-stitched on the back to conform to the curves and inside corners. Use a stiffer batting so the top edges don't sag, since the hanging casing must be applied below the lowest points along the top. 36" x 36" (91.5 x 91.5 cm)

Several quilts hung together in a grouping can be separated, overlapped, or attached with fabric or metal links. Color, theme, and/or technique should be unified in all the pieces. Your intent may be to show related images in different color schemes or to use the same colors for a range of designs, but the group should read as a whole. You might even make a large quilt and then cut it into sections and bind each separately.

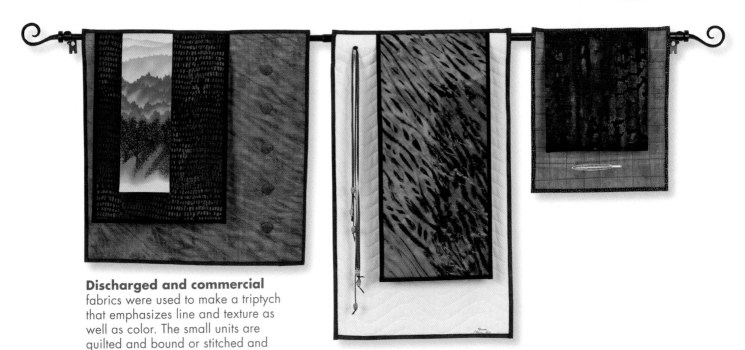

Discharged and commercial fabrics were used to make a triptych that emphasizes line and texture as well as color. The small units are quilted and bound or stitched and turned, with all the top edges tucked into a single binding. Discharged fabrics by Lucy Senstad and Susan Stein. 23" x 46" (58.5 x 117 cm)

To practice making a quilt with several parts, choose a large print fabric. Cut the fabric into three parts—equal in size or not. Place the pieces on the design wall and audition other fabrics and trims with them. Lightly fuse or pin the elements together, carrying some across all three panels for unity. When the panels are ready for stitching, pin everything thoroughly and take the panels to the sewing machine. Put batting behind the panels if you want to stitch and quilt at the same time. You can add backing if you want the stitching to show on the back of the quilt, or leave it off until the binding process. Stitch for stability, texture, and unity. After the stitching is complete, put the panels back on the design wall to see if they need more embellishment. Steam the panels if necessary, straighten the edges, and bind. Hang the pieces on a decorative rod or hang them as individual pieces with invisible hanging methods.

(continued)

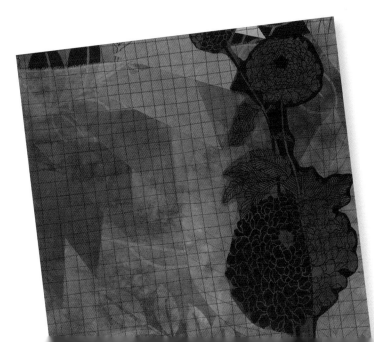

This three-part quilt is made from a black-and-white Alexander Henry print that has been overdyed. 24" x 44" (61 x 112 cm)

A quilt with a separated overlay makes a fascinating wall piece. The overlay might be separated from the back by ½" or 3" (1.5 or 7.5 cm) and might flutter in the breeze or be solid, even attached to a rigid framework. The overlay could be a sheer fabric, with or without designs on it, or could be a fabric with openings cut out of it. Some overlays are threadwork made on a dissolvable stabilizer. Choosing a format for your art quilt can lead you in all kinds of directions and even necessitate a little engineering knowledge along the way.

Made in a class with Katie Pasquini Masopust in 1983, this mandala shows an almost identical repeat block interpreted to look like sunrise, sunset, earth, and sky through the use of different color schemes. Quilting lines emphasize each theme. When the binding was added, an extra backing piece half the size of the back of the quilt was included. The bottom edge of the fabric was left loose, so a piece of foam core board could be inserted into the sleeve to maintain the round shape of the quilt. 20.5" (52 cm) diameter

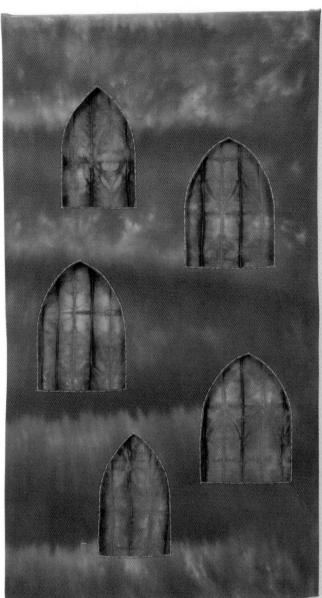

This piece is hung from a ¼" x ½" (6 x 15 mm) wood piece and resembles stained glass windows. Fabrics by Marit Lee Kucera and Judy Robertson. 39" x 21½" (99 x 54.5 cm)

Kit Eastman is the creator of this wonderful layered piece showing birds on both layers. A lightweight metal framework holds the overlay about 3" (7.5 cm) in front of the quilt. Kit specializes in fascinating printing techniques, including katazome, and she loves nature themes.
20" x 18" x 5" (51 x 45.5 x 12.5 cm)

This small piece shows a trim netting layer (sewn on Super Solvy) hanging over an overdyed decorator fabric that has been quilted and bound. The netting is tucked into the binding at the top and hangs free.
10¾" x 16" (27.5 x 40.5 cm)

Auditioning Techniques

Once a theme for a project has been chosen, it's time to audition techniques. Surface design on plain or subtly patterned fabrics is one option, while working with exciting artist-dyed or commercially printed fabrics is another. Traditional methods—either piecing or appliqué—are always options as is fusing, so common now but once a radical alternative! Sometimes the choice is simply a matter of your preferred way of working; sometimes a certain fabric must be used, as in the case of a group challenge project. It's fun to try a new technique seen in a book or magazine or to try the things learned in a class.

Include similar blocks in a small quilt, like this tie-dye sampler. Quilting by Sue Kelly. 47" x 58" (119.5 x 147.5 cm)

Doing a series of small studies can be a fun way to test techniques and products new to you. If they don't work, they can be discarded or used as backgrounds for other work, but often they prove to be good jumping-off places for a small collage or can be framed with a precut mat. Keep your pieces in a bin with other miscellaneous elements like orphan quilt blocks and purchased screen prints so they will be handy when inspiration strikes.

To start, look through your books and magazines or quilt show photos and make a list of the techniques you want to try. Work on small studies and then put them up on the design wall as you finish them. Some blocks will attract your eye and call for further consideration. Be sure to write notes on sticky labels and attach them to each sample so you have a record of what you did. If you build a collection of these studies, it's almost guaranteed you'll soon be teaching or demonstrating for your quilt group because these projects are fun to bring to show-and-tell and share with others.

YOU WILL NEED

- unflavored gelatin, four packets
- 2 cups (473 ml) water
- 8" or 9" (20.5 or 23 cm) cake pan
- plastic wrap
- opaque fabric paint
- sponge or foam brush
- fabric
- metal washers
- spray bottle
- iron

THEME: CIRCLES

Let's look at a number of techniques you might want to consider for your next (or first) art quilt. The theme is circles, an easy motif to work with, either using templates or making freehand cuts or brushstrokes. Circles are pleasing to look at, eliciting feelings of completeness and serenity. Of course, you could also make it your goal to present circles as startling and provocative designs! Art quilts are a blank canvas for expressing yourself, whatever your mood.

Gelatin Printing

Painting on fabric allows for maximum freedom in pattern design. Gelatin printing is a fun way to generate several versions of the same design.

1 Make a gelatin pad in a square cake pan by mixing four envelopes of unflavored gelatin with 1 cup (236.5 ml) of cold water. Add 1 cup (236.5 ml) of hot tap water, and chill until set. Tip the solid gelatin pad out of the pan onto plastic wrap.

2 Cover the surface of the pad with opaque paint using a small sponge or foam brush. Drop objects like washers onto the gelatin. Place a piece of fabric over the gelatin and rub over the back with your hands. Carefully peel the fabric off the surface.

3 Lift the washers off the gelatin and drop them, paint side down, onto a second piece of fabric. Press over the top of the objects to transfer the paint to the fabric.

4 Drop a third piece of fabric onto the surface of the gelatin and rub over the back. Peel the fabric off.

5 Spray the surface of the gelatin with a fine mist of water and take a fourth print from the remaining paint. Let the four samples dry and then iron to set the paint.

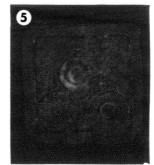

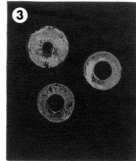

For an overall background of circles, sponge paint onto bubble wrap and stamp onto fabric. Or use the sponge to dab paint over sequin waste laid on the fabric. Do not attempt to make a perfect print in either case—the art is in the variations.

Find an orphan quilt block and try painting circles over the surface with a small brush and opaque paint. Here you can see the effect of using a dark blue watery paint first, which bled. The metallic paint covered completely but was difficult to apply smoothly over the bands of bias tape, which also would occur when painting over seam lines.

Painting with a sponge brush onto plain fabric is easy, but if you want to avoid white places, start with a colored fabric. An alternative is to paint the circles first with an opaque paint, let dry, and then do a wash of color with a transparent paint to fill in the background. Painting all three opaque colors at once allows the colors to mix for interesting combinations. Try using triad color schemes for a complex look.

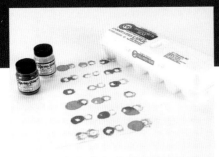  

Painting with things from around the house is fun, inexpensive, and creates great results. This piece was made by painting the bottom of a plastic egg carton with watery paint and then pressing it onto the fabric. Two prints were made next to each other for interest.

A meat tray was used to make a negative print (one where the background prints, not the image itself). The edges of the tray were removed to create a flat sheet of foam into which circles were inscribed with a ballpoint pen. Metallic paint was sponged onto the foam and turned facedown on the fabric and rubbed to transfer the paint. Work quickly to avoid having the paint dry on the foam instead of printing on the fabric.

PVC pipe, foam pipe insulation, and a stamp made from a sheet of thin foam adhered to a piece of foam core board were used to make this sample with metallic paint.

Round sponges of several sizes were used to make circular patterns, but in this case, the watery paint bled too much and obliterated the design. This sample might be relegated to the discard or background pile.

Water-soluble crayons were used to make circles on white fabric. Afterward, the fabric was sprayed with water and then black spray paint to fill in the white spaces and make the crayon bleed.

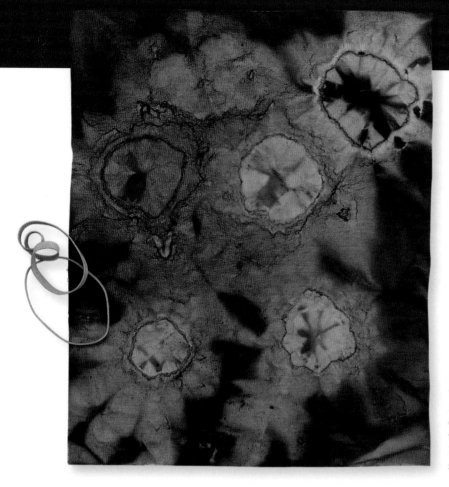

Rubber bands were used to make tie-dye circles on this sample. Watery paint poured on the dampened fabric allowed two colors to bleed and blend together to make interesting variations in color and serendipitous patterns.

These tie-dye samples lead us into dyeing techniques. Here the circles were made by stitching and gathering the fabric and then dipping it in dye. The tightly pulled up stitches kept the color lighter in those areas and provided intricate detail.

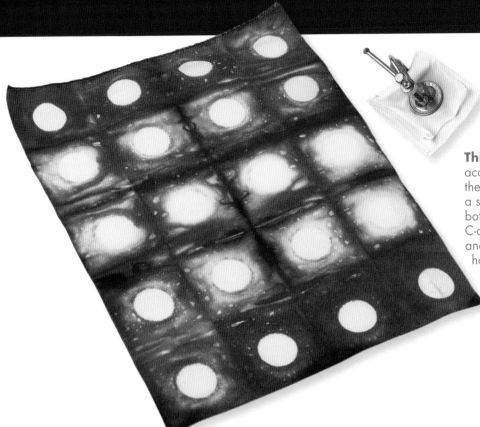

This fabric was folded into accordion pleats the long way and then was accordion folded to form a square. Quarters were placed on both sides of the folded fabric and C-clamped tightly, squirted with dye, and put into a baggie for twenty-four hours. Interesting variations resulted, depending on the position of each section in the folded stack.

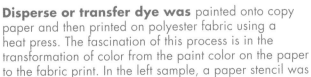

Disperse or transfer dye was painted onto copy paper and then printed on polyester fabric using a heat press. The fascination of this process is in the transformation of color from the paint color on the paper to the fabric print. In the left sample, a paper stencil was laid between the fabric and the painted paper when they were placed in the heat press so the color would not transfer where the stencil was. The disadvantage to this method is that it requires the use of synthetic fabric, which can be harder to handle.

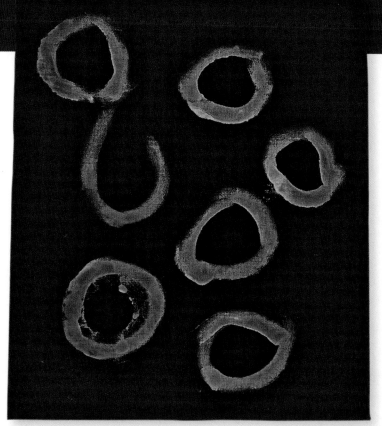

Taking dye out of the fabric
is yet another way to create circles. Simply painting discharge paste onto dark fabric, letting it dry, and then ironing it with a steam iron removes the color from the fabric. Besides brushing the paste on the fabric, as was done in the sample, you could also stamp, screen print, or stencil it on.

A plastic shape template with circles of different sizes was used to paint discharge paste onto a patchwork scrap done with hand-dyed fabric. After ironing, the discharged area of the fabric is a beautiful color and contrasts well with the background. Discharge paste or bleach discharge should always be tested, because various fabrics will react differently. Remember that paste will work on lots of fibers while bleach products will only work on cotton, rayon, and linen.

The discharged circles on the fabric in this sample were distorted by sewing the fabric to Texture Magic, a product that shrinks when a steam iron is held over it. Discharged fabric by Lucy Senstad.

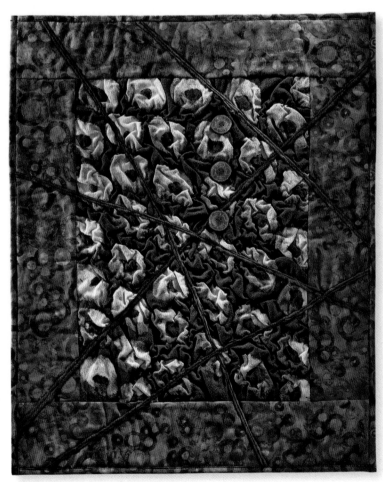

Xs and Os. **The textured** discharge sample above was made into a small finished wall hanging by adding a border and couching yarn over the top. Handmade polymer buttons provide the finishing touch. 17½" x 21¾" (44.5 x 55.5 cm)

Hand- or machine-stitched techniques are myriad and can also be auditioned. The point is to try anything that piques your interest. Sometimes it is fun to ask a friend over to try different techniques and play the "what if?" game while exploring lots of possibilities. Keep notes and files of samples—sometimes a technique that doesn't interest you right now turns out to be the perfect answer to a design dilemma down the road.

These techniques are just a sampling of the many ways that you can generate designs on cloth. Think about what comes after the creation of the quilt top—will you embellish with beading, heavy stitching, couching of yarns, felting, or some other method that will be affected by what is underneath? It is difficult to hand-stitch through heavy paint or thick fused layers, so keep the quilt top soft for those finishing approaches. The impact you want for the theme motif can influence your choice—is the motif simply an interesting background pattern or is it the main emphasis for the quilt? Can't decide where to go next? Use some of the studies to go a step further, auditioning layering, embellishing, or stitching. You are doing the work and growing with each step in the process. Eventually you will find your own voice and style.

Of course, you can always start with commercial fabric. Choose fabrics that have high contrast and iron fusible web to the back of small pieces. Freehand cut, or use a template to cut circles out of the fusible-backed fabric. Peel the release paper off the back of the fabric pieces and iron them to a background.

Part of a year-long challenge project, this piece employs fused free-cut circular shapes. The center area is filled in with a beaded star design. 11" x 20" (28 x 51 cm)

Selecting Fabric

Since most art quilts reside on the wall, they can be made of unusual materials that would not stand up to regular handling or washing. Fabrics and trims should not deteriorate with age but can be somewhat delicate. They can also be quite stiff since the piece will not be handled.

Think of everything as fair game—cheesecloth, candy wrappers, old chiffon scarves, papers of all kinds, Tyvek (used as a moisture barrier on new houses and for postal envelopes), interfacings, and a thousand other things contribute texture and interest to a wall piece. Remember that art quilts for the wall differ from other quilts because they will be seen from a distance and then examined from close up and are seen vertically instead of laid on a couch or bed. Maintain the viewer's interest with a variety of materials, techniques, and details.

Cotton is usually the fabric of choice for most quilts. It handles beautifully, sews easily, comes in thousands of colors and patterns, and can be dyed or painted effortlessly in the home studio. Hand-dyers create fabulous fabrics and coordinated bundles to tempt us at shows and online. Many times a lovely bundle of hand-dyed fat quarters is all the inspiration a quilter needs to start a new project. Cotton even lets go of its color with the application of bleach products or discharge paste. Grocery-store cheesecloth, which can be colored anything you like, is a great addition to many pieces. For a slightly heavier gauze, look for cotton curtain scrim in the drapery department of the fabric store.

Wool is very popular with art quilters and traditional quilters alike. Since it can be shrunk down to a point where it won't ravel, appliqué enthusiasts love it. It comes in many weights, so it can be used for piecing as well. Hand-dyers like to find old wool blankets and color them in beautiful shibori patterns and then bead or embroider designs over them.

Silk in many weights works well for art quilts—the thin, slippery ones can be ironed to a knit interfacing for body and ease of handling, and the thick ones can be butted against each other for zigzag sewing to avoid bulky seams. Silk dupioni is a favorite fabric of many fiber artists for its sheen and gorgeous colors. This assortment of fabrics includes a remnant from a silk tie factory, a silk/rayon velvet devore, and an overdyed vintage kimono piece.

Wendie Zekowski's piece shows how gorgeous a thrift store blanket can become in an artist's hands! 16" x 31½" (40.5 x 80 cm)

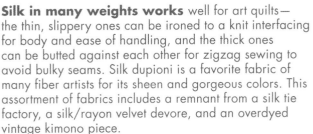

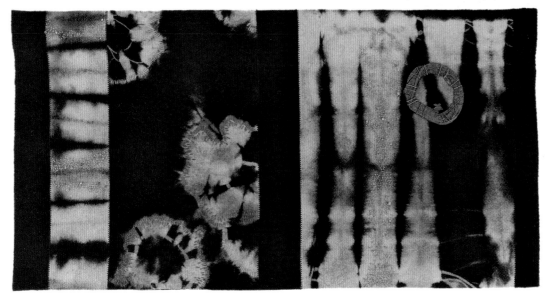

Odd fabrics like upholstery and drapery fabrics work well for art quilts, and some artists dye over light-colored decorator fabrics to give them one-of-a-kind appeal. Using fabrics of different weights does not matter in an art quilt like it does with a traditional pieced bed quilt where a heavy fabric might put stress on a thinner one. Overdyed fabric by Wendy Richardson.

Wendy Richardson made this piece using an overdyed vintage napkin and various overdyed decorator fabrics. She dyed rayon twill tape to match her fabrics and added it with French knots. Handmade blanket stitches around the leaves add texture, and small buttons on top of metal washers embellish the surface along with machine stitching along the lines of the damask napkin. 14½" x 14" (37 x 35.5 cm)

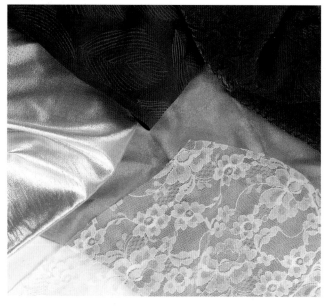

Don't overlook synthetics like faux suede and metallics. Some polyesters are gorgeous and there are no prohibitions to using them. Sheers of silk, nylon, and polyester—the thinner the better—are essential for layering.

> Nature will bear the closest inspection. She invites us to lay our eye level with her smallest leaf, and take an insect view of the plain. Henry David Thoreau

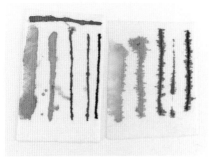

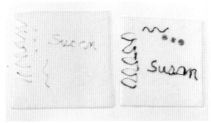

Lutradur is a nonwoven material that comes in different weights and can be painted, dyed, printed on, and burned. Since it doesn't ravel, fancy edges and patterns can be cut or melted into it with heat guns and tools. Tyvek can be melted into wild textures with an iron held close to the surface and painted before or after heating.

Heavy interfacings can also be cut with a heat tool and colored with paint. All these materials are extremely durable, so think of them for making books and vessels.

Part of a challenge series, this piece shows Dye-na-Flow—painted Lutradur that has been burned with a heat tool (like a soldering iron). A leaf photo printed on organza is layered over the Lutradur, and the Mistyfuse web that is exposed after the tree and leaves are applied is foiled to look like frost. 10" x 20" (25.5 x 51 cm)

Even the crunchy felt made from recycled milk bottles melts in interesting ways using a heat gun to make holes or a soldering iron to cut shapes or edges. Make sure to take the proper safety precautions when melting any synthetic materials, as they release fumes.

Part of another challenge series is this quilt, which is covered with heat-gun-distressed felt. The background fabric is decorated with painted Wonder-Under, so the felt fuses to it easily; use a piece of cooking parchment paper over the top to protect the iron. 11" x 20" (28 x 51 cm)

Found papers, tissue paper, old photos, even magazine clippings can end up in cloth/paper lamination or layered pieces where they are covered with glue or sheer fabric. Paper/cloth lamination is a process of layering sheers and papers with trims and holding them together with diluted glue or fluid acrylic medium.

Art supply stores have gorgeous papers from all over the world. Collect a few sheets and you'll find them the perfect material for adding to a collage. Many are quite durable, and the transparent or lacy ones are great for layering. Even a woven newspaper placemat becomes a potential fabric.

A piece of handmade paper inlaid with leaves was the starting point for this piece. Tiny squares of curtain scrim were cut and then sewn back together, raveling all the way! Pieces of sheer colored fabric were fused to the paper and a cutout cotton tree was fused over the sheers. The scrim layer was fused over the top and all the edges were left raw. For display, this piece could be attached to mat board and framed. 25" x 36" (63.5 x 91.5 cm)

The matted piece here is done with a copy of a scrapbooking cutout on organza, commercial and hand-painted fabric, handmade paper, watercolor crayon on rice paper, and paper leaves. 13¾" x 10¾" (35 x 27.5 cm)

If you still need more options, try making your own fabric! Weaving strips of any type of fabric or paper makes a fascinating and complex surface to further embellish. Remember that nylon sheers, like the ones in the sample, melt easily, so turn the iron down. Lay out a set of parallel strips on a piece of thin fusible batting, fusible web, or even silver lamé with Mistyfuse attached to it and tape one end to the table. Weave more strips through the first strips until the piece is complete and then iron to stabilize.

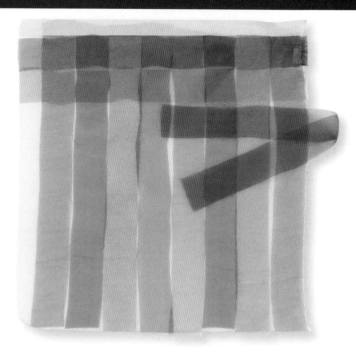

The weaving was covered with a photo printed onto silk net organza and fused with Mistyfuse web. Beading or stitching could be added to make the piece even more unique. 10¾" x 12½" (27.5 x 32 cm)

Two silk fusion pieces with
almost identical elements look
different when sewn to contrasting
or coordinating backgrounds. The
embellishments either highlight the
silk pieces or relegate them more to
the background.
A: 12½" x 16" (32 x 40.5 cm)
B: 17¾" x 13½" (45 x 34.5 cm)

Using wool roving to
needle felt or wet felt is great fun.
Needle felting can be done by
machine for quick results, using either
a machine attachment or a special
sewing machine with no bobbin and
multiple needles. In the sample, a
stencil was laid on the background
and roving was hand-needled around
the edges of the design. The stencil
was removed and the leaf was
then filled in with a needle-felting
attachment on the sewing machine.
This piece could be used as a
foundation for further embellishment.

Silk roving can be used to
make silk paper or fusion, using
textile medium as an adhesive. Silk
fiber with the sericin from the cocoon
still in it can simply be ironed into a
flat sheet of fiber.

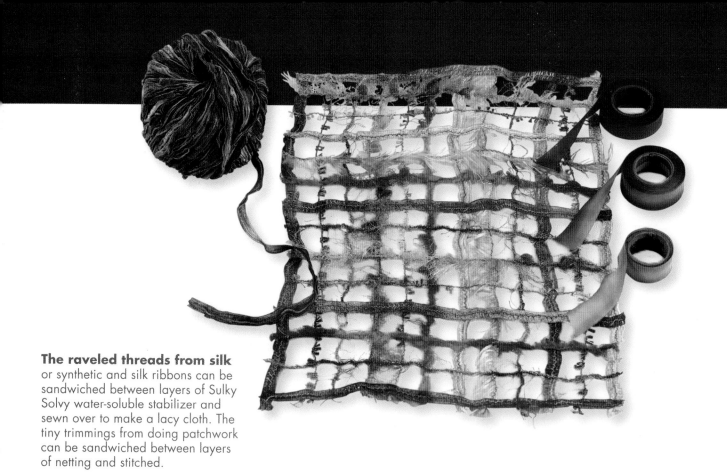

The raveled threads from silk
or synthetic and silk ribbons can be
sandwiched between layers of Sulky
Solvy water-soluble stabilizer and
sewn over to make a lacy cloth. The
tiny trimmings from doing patchwork
can be sandwiched between layers
of netting and stitched.

Even metal is making its way
into the art quilter's stash. Copper
sheeting, foil, mesh, and screen all
sew to fabric easily using a sewing
machine. Heavier metals can be
punched with holes and hand-
stitched. Heating the copper with a
torch, candle, or heat gun transforms
its color to beautiful reds and blues.
Spraying it with vinegar or liver of
sulfur makes it black or mottled, and
painting it with alcohol inks can
make it any color. Soaking copper
in bleach colors and eats holes in it
while adding turquoise highlights.

Real leaves were temporarily adhered to copper screen, and liver of sulfur was sprayed over it. The screen was then sprayed with artist's fixative to preserve the colors, and bias tape was used to enclose the edges and sew the metal to the wall hanging.

A sampler of copper techniques shows how bleach, vinegar, candle flame, and heat gun affect the color of the metal. An ordinary needle in the sewing machine was used to attach the metal to the quilt.

By now it's clear that anything goes in an art quilt, as long as it can be successfully integrated into the design. Look everywhere for fabric, including the art store, hardware store, and home improvement store. Good composition and construction are the guides to what will work—there are no rules. Just be prepared for the ever-popular question "But how do you wash it?" to which your answer is "I don't."

Using a Sketchbook

Another approach to starting a new project is the sketchbook. Some artists keep theirs with them wherever they go, in case an interesting idea or motif presents itself. All kinds of design decisions can be worked out before ever touching a piece of fabric—simply draw options in the sketchbook, color them, and revisit them from time to time, revising them as you wish.

Use pencil to sketch ideas and thoughts into the sketchbook. If blank white pages are intimidating, paint a transparent wash over the pages, making sure the paper will withstand the use of water-based mediums first. After a design is sketched, go over the lines with a permanent marker for definition and then use watercolor paint, colored pencils, or Paintstiks to fill in. The advantage to working this way instead of making small fabric studies is that you can carry your sketchbook wherever you go and jot down ideas whenever inspiration strikes. No fabric is wasted, although you may want to glue tiny swatches of fabric to your sketchbook and carry them with you when shopping for fabric. Nothing draws a crowd faster than opening a lovely sketchbook in a shop.

Karen Wallach's sketchbooks are beautiful to look through and keep her focused during meetings too! A tiny kit of pens, pencils, watercolor paint, water bottle, and water-filled brush goes with the sketchbook, so she is ready to create at any time. Pages can be extended by gluing on additional paper for larger sketches. Every person will have their favorite format for a sketchbook—large or small, stitched or spiral, vertical or horizontal in shape. Here Karen has sketches of helping her friend can apples and the apples themselves, which will become the focus for her quilt.

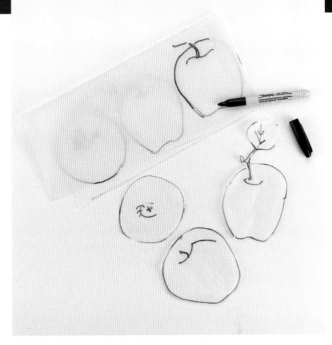

An enlargement of the design in Karen's sketchbook serves as the pattern for the quilt. Heavy black outlines make the design easy to see and trace. Karen advises that drawing with a solid line rather than short sketchy marks makes the transformation to sewing easier—she calls it "a commitment to the line."

If you want to expand on the drawing, fold over the paper and trace another element, or tear the design apart and tape the parts to a larger piece of paper.

The finished piece shows the translation from idea in the sketchbook to art quilt. The design may change through the course of construction, but Karen knows where she is headed when she begins to audition fabric. If you like, tape the pattern directly to the fabric and stitch through it and then rip it off afterward. Karen tapes the pattern in front of her machine so she can refer to it and sew freehand. She says that if you can't sew a straight line, make all your lines crooked or "design to your faults."
Photo by Petronella J. Ytsma

Working in a Series

Many art quilters find that working in a series helps them develop an idea and build a body of work. Rather than reinventing the wheel every time they want to make a new piece, they simply add to an already developed group of quilts—they don't need to decide on a theme or style. Even if the series is a personally assigned challenge to do one small piece a week or month for a year, you will be surprised how your artistic voice comes out through repetition and variation.

If you use a sketchbook, your kernels of ideas will probably flow through a lot of the pages. If you are a person who works directly with the fabric to start a design, picking one fabric to base a series on may work for you. Or choose a theme that interests you and that you know will hold your attention. You might want to make lists of possible themes and techniques.

For a year-long challenge project with friends, my start was making a list of faith-based words that would be represented each month. The second list was possible techniques for each piece. Then twelve pieces of background fabric were prepared—either with painting or fusing—so that there was a ready-made starting point each month. All the backgrounds were prepared to match the common challenge fabric that everyone was to use for the year. Whenever the time or mood presented itself, a background was taken out of the pile and a topic was chosen from the list. A technique that would work for that topic was selected and the fun began. All pieces in the series are 11" x 20" (28 x 51 cm).

What makes this series work is the common color scheme and, of course, the style of the work. There is a visual cohesiveness throughout. Different fabrics and techniques are used, but it is obvious the pieces go together even without the wave running through them.

The first piece (Salvation) started with a commercial batik that Paintstik was applied to, using a rubber rug gripper underneath to enable a grid pattern to be rubbed on the fabric. A ribbon weaving was done on water-soluble stabilizer, rinsed, and sewn to the background. The theme fabric was used as an insert, starting a wave that would run through all the pieces.

The second piece (Praise) was a commercial batik with painted Wonder-Under fusible web applied to it. A piece of synthetic felt was ironed to the Wonder-Under after being distressed with a heat gun. Again, the theme fabric was run through the quilt, matching the curve of the first piece. A flat paper and polymer clay doll was glued in place.

The third quilt (Forgiveness) started as a piece of white fabric that was painted with Dye-na-Flow transparent paint and lots of water. Sheer, hand-dyed fabrics were layered over the background and parallel lines of stitching were sewn over the whole piece. Again, the insert was added as well as an enamel button.

Fourth in the series (Prayer) was based on a screen-printed background (the screen was patterned with masking tape). Hand-dyed fabrics in a run from muted rose to green were stitched in rows with faux script. "Lines of communication" made from ribbon and trim go up and down.

The fifth quilt (Love) began with a commercial batik fabric covered with painted cheesecloth adhered with Mistyfuse. Cutout pieces of fabric were fused in a circular pattern, and stitching was added for detail and durability. Hand-beading was done in the middle of the circle, and an agate was added to echo the circular focus.

Mercy was portrayed with four offset layers of black tulle on a background painted with rug gripper underneath to create a faint grid. Gold lines were stitched from the light areas downward and a Thermofax screen was used to print a row of abstract people for the bottom area.

Warm sun melts the grip
of the winter's ice and snow,
Wind blows in spring's kiss.

You may not be making a series that is this time and theme related; nonetheless, you will likely find that the more quilts you make, the more they start to look like you. It is always a good idea to show your work in a trusted group and ask for critique. There are formal ways to conduct critical response if your group is interested, but an informal showing of several pieces at once can also elicit comments that will highlight your strong points and point you toward paths in your work you might want to develop more fully. You might not even realize you have a series going until you see your quilts displayed together in one place.

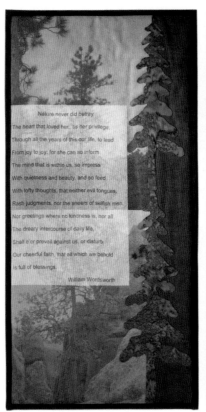

Nature never did betray
The heart that loved her, 'tis her privilege,
Through all the years of this our life, to lead
From joy to joy, for she can so inform
The mind that is within us, so impress
With quietness and beauty, and so feed
With lofty thoughts, that neither evil tongues,
Rash judgments, nor the sneers of selfish men,
Nor greetings where no kindness is, nor all
The dreary intercourse of daily life,
Shall e'er prevail against us, or disturb
Our cheerful faith, that all which we behold
Is full of blessings.
William Wordsworth

Twelve 10" by 20"
(25.5 x 51 cm) quilts make up a series done in 2010. Each month's background is a color of the color wheel and the theme is trees. Photo transfer on fabric was the main technique used and was more successfully integrated in some pieces than others. Again, there is visual cohesiveness to the grouping because of theme and technique. The varied colors, if viewed in succession, also form a pattern.

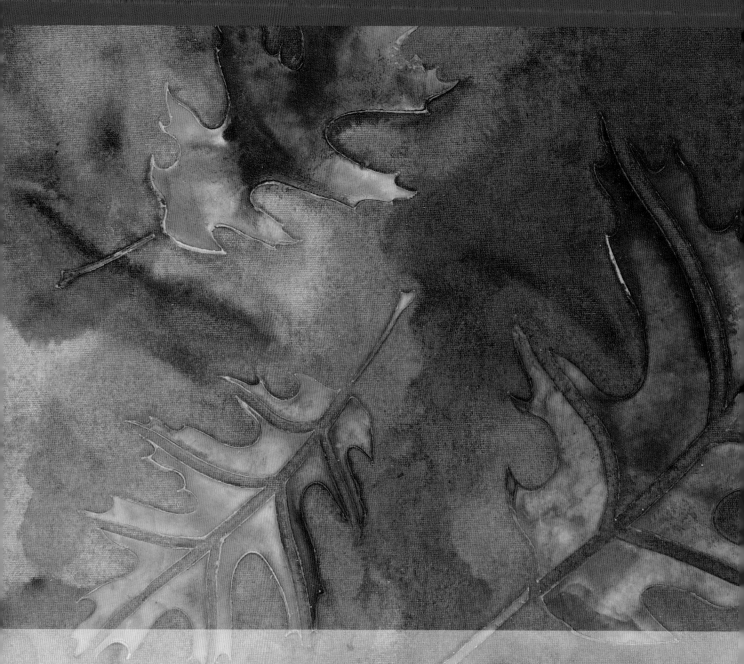

DESIGN ELEMENTS

Knowing a few basics about design can make creating art quilts a little easier. How often have you tried to put different fabrics together or tried to make a collage and found that it didn't look quite right? Realizing that variations in value or an asymmetrical arrangement are needed can make all the difference. It's even a valuable exercise to work through a design book with a few friends and see what different approaches emerge when everyone's work is shown together. Learning in the abstract is one thing, but seeing actual work and discussing a variety of interpretations can be truly eye-opening.

Lines

While there are variations in the way design elements and principles are defined, all artists follow basic guidelines to create good art, ones that apply to prehistoric cave paintings and to our work today.

Designs are built around lines, which are defined as a series of dots—something that is longer than it is wide. Lines sometimes enclose shapes or they may stand alone; sometimes they convey mood and emotion. Horizontal lines are calming, vertical ones imply the possibility of motion, and diagonal lines imply action.

The eye naturally follows a line, and artists use them as a vehicle to keep the viewer moving around a piece of art. In landscapes, a horizontal line usually indicates a horizon, and parallel lines that converge toward the top of the picture indicate a road or river receding into the distance.

Lines can vary considerably, even though they are always longer than they are wide. Here is an assortment of lines cut from fabric. How do their differences affect the way you respond to them? Do any suggest landscape, sky features, anger, happiness? Notice how the lines in the background fabric add more interest than a plain piece of fabric.

Make a small piece with a striped background and simple fused lines. The ones in this sample are placed asymmetrically in a grid pattern. Turn your piece in different directions—you might see a Japanese gate, a building under construction, or the windows of an apartment building. The lines of gold stitching might represent rain or, if they all came from a common point, the sun's rays. Using a binding fabric with lines makes an interesting edge. In quilting, lines become a very real element because they appear in the fabric, the pattern, and the stitching.

A charming stitched book made by Damaris Jackson illustrates just how expressive a single line can be!

Value

Value is another design element that vitally influences how a piece will look. It is defined as the lightness or darkness of a color, and some people say that value is more important than the color of a fabric. Monochromatic color schemes (those using one color in several values) are very powerful and are being used more and more in contemporary quilting.

Here a bundle of carefully dyed fabrics in eight values has been used to create a simple but dramatic quilt with visual dimensionality. 52" x 45" (132 x 114.5 cm)

This piece illustrates how pairing brightly colored fabrics with black-and-white elements creates a dynamic effect. The text on the white rectangles invites a closer view of the quilt and, by its sentiments, calms the excitement generated by the harsh color contrasts. 34½" x 10¼" (87.5 x 26 cm)

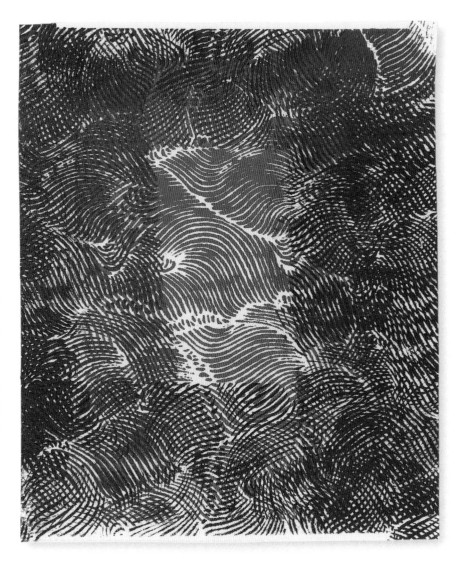

Value in art quilting may differ from what is used in traditional quilting, because sharp value differences are more dramatic. There are fewer pastels and muted or grayed colors used, probably because the artist is making something for the wall and not to match a bedroom or sofa. High contrast attracts the eye.

Screen printing three values of red paint onto white fabric illustrates how simply depth can be created. The lightest value was printed first.

Color

Color is likely the most intimidating element to the beginning quilter, yet it is the most fun to play with and master.

Colors have emotional context and there are many phrases that refer to color, like "I feel blue today," "I'm seeing red," "I'm in the pink," or "green with envy." Notice the colors used in doctor's offices, hospitals, concert halls, restaurants—all designed to set a mood. It's important to remember that color theory won't help you design your next project unless you actually take out the paints or fabrics and play with them so the concepts become real.

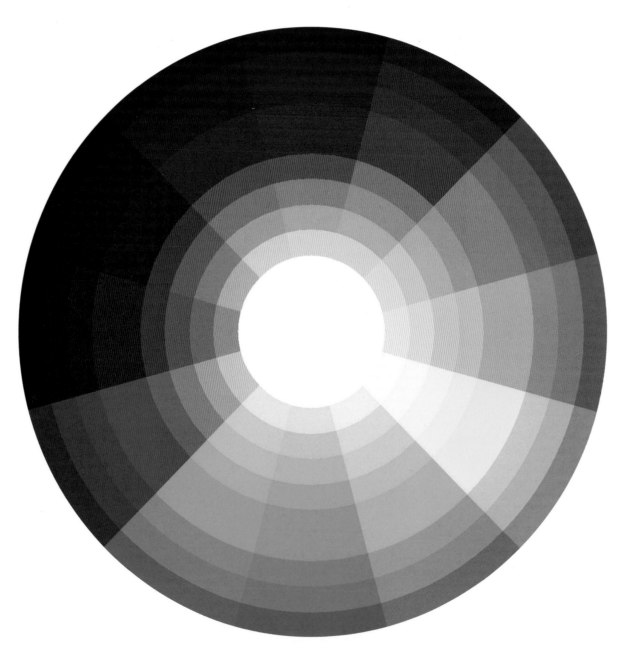

Look at the color wheel,
either a six-step or twelve-step.
Colors opposite each other are
called complementary and will
make an exciting artwork. Red and
green, blue and orange, or violet
and yellow, for instance, are used
for sports teams for a reason, since
the goal is to generate excitement
when a game is being played.
It is interesting to note that when
complementary colors are mixed,
the end result is brown; it is fun to
experiment with diluted paint to see
what mixtures you can make.

This fabric contains violet, red, and orange so it's bright but not too powerful because the colors are related and there is low contrast between them.

Analogous colors are next to each other on the color wheel, and it's easy to make a successful project when you use them.

Triadic colors make a complex and rich looking piece. They lie at equal distances at three points around the color wheel. The primaries of yellow, blue, and red are the most commonly thought of triadic colors, but violet, green, and orange are very popular when used in variations of the pure colors, like dark plum, moss green, and rust. Of course, everyone has a different idea of what plum looks like—color is very subjective and people will perceive it in many ways.

This piece of fabric by
Diane Swallen has the three triadic primaries—blue, red, and yellow—but due to the manipulation of the fabric and the blending of the dyes, orange, green, violet, and brown also appear.

Be aware that there are two sets of primary colors—one used in painting and one in printing. Painter's primaries are red, blue, and yellow. Printer's primaries are magenta, turquoise, and yellow, which make vibrant violet and green. Make a simple color wheel by mixing paint in both primary sets, painting it onto paper, and cutting pie-shaped slices. Depending on the "temperature" of the piece you are making, you may want to choose the cooler printer's primaries or the warmer painter's primaries. You can also create temperature differences by staying on one side of the color wheel or the other.

The proportion of orange to the other colors makes orange the dominant, or major, color in this fabric swatch.

Orange in six different values makes a mono–chromatic color scheme. If white were added to the bright orange, it would be called a tint. If black were added, it would be a shade of orange. Here, the dye is increased in proportion to the water used so there is a gain in intensity of color but not a change in the color's property.

Orange is the accent, or minor, color in this section of the same fabric because the other colors are proportionately greater.

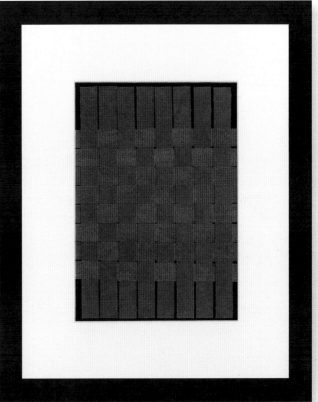

The colors next to orange on the color wheel are red-orange and yellow-orange. Using the three of them together will make a bright but pleasing combination and visually reduce the usual impact that orange has on the eye.

The complement to orange is blue and combining the two pure colors will create vibrations! Remember this if your art quilt needs a little pepping up—just a little of the complementary color will help. For a fun exercise, stare at a bright blue object for a while and then look at a white piece of paper. You will see orange! The afterimage of any color is its complement.

The triadic colors that go with orange are violet and green. Remember that the colors don't have to be used in equal amounts. Start noticing how many fabrics include variations of triadic combinations—they are rich and inviting.

Texture

Texture is another design element that becomes very real to the art quilter, since fabric pattern, thread, stitching, batting, surface design, manipulation of materials, and embellishment all create visual or actual structural changes to the quilt's surface.

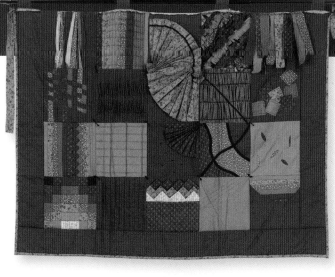

From the earliest age, when babies fondle the satin edge on their blankets, people love texture in everything from furnishings to food. These paper swatches show actual texture (variations in the surface can be felt with the hand) and visual texture (flat paper is printed with a design that looks like a woven material).

This faded quilt was my first attempt at creating more texture in a quilt. It was made in 1983, when everything had to be straight and tidy, but after seeing a weaving exhibit where the weavings were 3" (7.5 cm) thick, I set out to make quilts with texture. I was a little before my time though, because the person hanging a show that included my quilt called to ask if I realized it wasn't finished! 28" x 35" (71 x 89 cm)

Texture is a good device for making a piece interesting from close up, after the viewer has enjoyed the quilt from a distance. Heavy quilting is often used around a painted whole-cloth motif to fill in the background and add interest.

Add texture to fabric using a stencil and modeling paste. The paste will create a design that's raised above the surface. After the paste dries, wash over the fabric with a watery paint and place the piece on top of a small stretched canvas to keep the paste from cracking through handling. Cover the edges of the fabric and stretched canvas with glued-on copper foil.

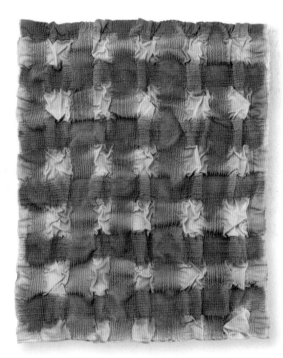

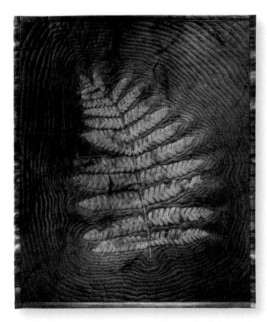

Here a sun print is surrounded by echo quilting for texture and to pop up the fern. Sun print by Diane Bartels. 17½" x 20¾" (44.5 x 53 cm)

Two pieces of fabric cut from the same half-yard (0.46 m) illustrate how far texture can go. One is quilted with a variegated thread that gives it as much visual texture as actual texture because the lines of stitching add a secondary design to the piece. The second piece is heavily textured (and shrunk) by sewing it to Solvron, a water-soluble stabilizer. Heavy stitching is not as noticeable as the shrinkage and puckering that occur when the stabilizer is only partially dissolved.

Balance

Balance is usually an easy design concept to grasp because when we look at a quilt we're working on, it will tell us whether it's right or not.

Though visual balance may be a bit trickier than figuring out how to balance an armful of books, it becomes pretty obvious if we regularly hang all our work on the design wall. Formal, or symmetrical balance, is what traditional quilting is built on—a grid layout of the blocks, which are also built around a grid plan.

Informal balance is asymmetrical—both sides of the design are not the same but there is still a sense of balance because different elements have equal visual weight. I call this principle "planned randomness," and we quilters spend a lot of time making things look scattered and casual. Looking through a reducing glass or the wrong side of binoculars can help with assessing balance, because the design pieces are reduced to value and shape rather than busy fabric patterns or textures.

Cut squares of different fabrics in various color values and sizes. Choose a background fabric and place it on the design wall. Audition lots of arrangements of the squares to see how value, color, size, and arrangement all affect the balance of the piece. Take a digital photo of each version, download the photos into a computer program like Photoshop, and print out a contact sheet of all the choices. Do any of the designs feel "off balance?"

This quilt top certainly isn't matching on both sides, either vertically or horizontally, but the intensity of color and contrast in the pieced blocks balance the dynamic of the batik masks.

Unity

Unity is the last of the design elements in our study. One of the first things an art quilter has to master is how to tie all the parts of a piece together, since there is no printed pattern or traditional design to follow. Unity is the sum of all the design elements and comes with practice and maturity, giving the viewer a sense of completeness.

Sometimes the background of a piece can help create unity by repeating a pattern over the surface. Rather than choosing a solid color fabric, think about using a textured or printed fabric.

Repeating an element of the design can unify a quilt, carrying the viewer's eye around the piece. You can, however, have a totally unified piece that becomes boring. Remember to add a focal point to the quilt through embellishment, appliqué, or fiber art jewelry (a small ornament, button, or bead). Otherwise, your quilt may look like an unfinished background.

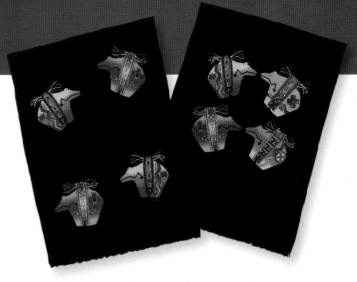

Simply putting images closer together can create unity, as shown in these samples.

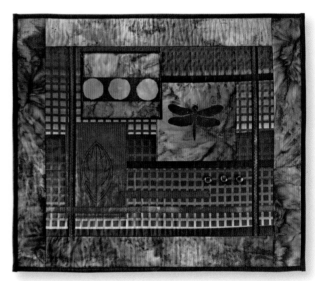

This collage works because the background fabric contains a unifying grid and also suggests the colors used throughout the piece. Background fabric by Lunn Fabrics. 24¾" x 21¼" (63 x 54 cm)

Here the fabric repeats the lines of color and the stitching supports the linear look of the fabric. Fabric by Liz Axford. 11½" x 12" (29 x 30.5 cm)

K. Eastman '09

CREATING THE ART QUILT TOP

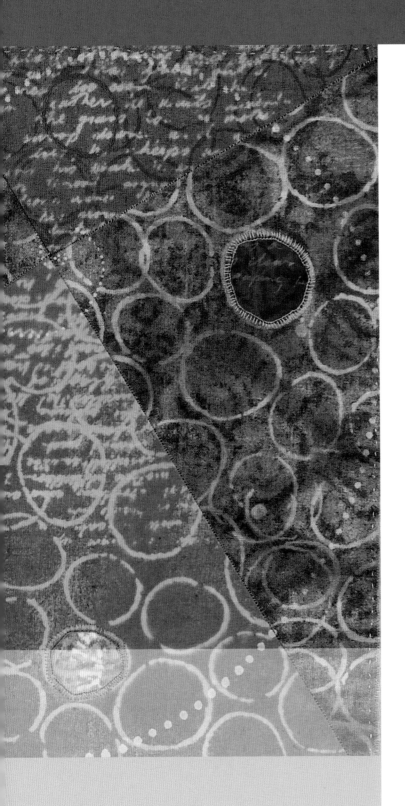

There really is no way to write "the complete photo guide" to art quilting because art quilts are by definition one of a kind and each artist has a different style. This section gives the beginning art quilter an easy entry point into a very exciting world. Once you have done some of the projects shown here, you will be able to take off on your own and challenge yourself to make truly original pieces. The projects here illustrate how simply an art quilt can start out, to be finished with stitching and embellishment. Whatever your interests are, there is a style that will fit and a method of working that will appeal. The most important thing is to start! Work small, make lots of pieces, and don't expect all of them to be masterpieces.

Quilt by Kit Eastman

Options

You've decided to make an art quilt. You might think about starting with a piece of fabric, using a sketchbook where you've been developing ideas, drawing a detailed plan on paper, designing on the computer, starting with a photograph, developing a theme prescribed for you or from your head, being inspired by a piece of art in a gallery or museum, or making a statement—controversial or not. Only you know where you'll start, and your way of working may change over time.

In this section, you'll see different approaches being used by art quilters to portray different subjects or images. These ideas represent a tiny fraction of the possibilities open to you as you explore the wide world of art quilting. Not so long ago, quilts were only for beds and followed prescribed patterns. Today, we can have so much fun expressing ourselves in a medium we are familiar with and which other people relate to.

Remember that an art quilt can be as small as a fabric postcard, so play with ideas and techniques on a small scale before committing to a large wall hanging. Keep notes and samples so you can recall what worked well and organize your work space to make creating a pleasure. If you like dyeing or painting fabric, make a stash of pieces so they are ready to go when inspiration strikes. When shopping, keep your eyes open for interesting additions—fabric, trims, embellishments, and beads. It is frustrating to know what you want for your quilt and find that the store where you saw it no longer has it. Of course, quilt conferences are the treasure trove of raw materials, so try to attend one at least once a year. If you're a recycler, you're already stashing things (ideally in an organized way!) to use later because you *know* you'll never get another chance to collect that item.

The quilt tops shown may be created in a different way from what you are used to doing. If the piece is small, you can make a collaged or appliquéd top with the batting attached to the back of the fabric while you work. Fusible batting can be steam ironed to the background fabric, so it is stabilized and so some of the quilting happens while you are topstitching or appliquéing fabrics in place. The backing will be added after the rest of the quilting and the embellishing is completed. By leaving the backing off until the end of the process, you can bring the backing fabric around to the front and make an easy and attractive binding, after trimming the quilt to perfect dimensions. It is just one way of working. You may prefer quilting to show on the back of the quilt or you may be a person who enjoys hand-stitching the binding to the back of the quilt. Different finishing approaches will be shown at the end of the book.

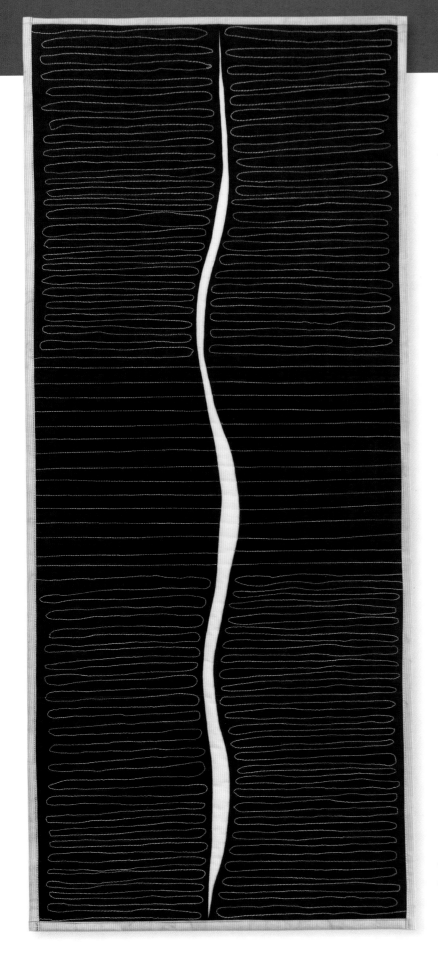

Lines

Just as the Design Elements section began with an exploration of lines, this construction section also begins with a look at lines because they are essential to any design and simple to make. Rigid or casual, lines are full of possibilities. The wall quilts in this chapter highlight lines as a motif.

This piece illustrates how effectively one line can create a focal point, value contrast, movement, balance, and unity. 12½" x 30" (32 x 76 cm)

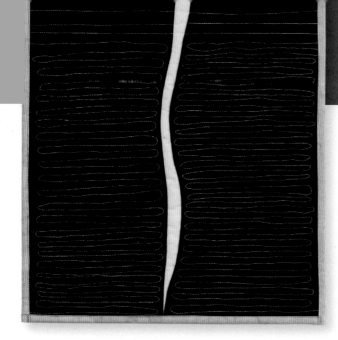

SINGLE LINE

1 To begin a line quilt, choose two fabrics that contrast with each other, usually in color and value. Cut the main fabric to slightly larger than the size of the finished piece, making it longer than it is wide. Most wall hangings that do not have borders or rigid patterns can be worked on a little larger piece and trimmed after the quilting is done to ensure perfect measurements.

2A For an inserted line, like the sample quilt, rotary-cut a wavy line through the middle of the main fabric. Turn under the edges on both sides of the cut, making some parts of the line wider and some narrower. Trim away excess fabric in the wide parts so the seam allowances turn easily. Place a contrast fabric strip underneath the opening between the main fabric pieces, and pin it in place. Hand or machine-appliqué both edges of the main fabric to the contrast strip.

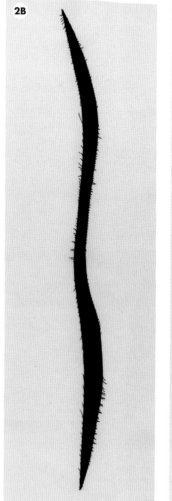

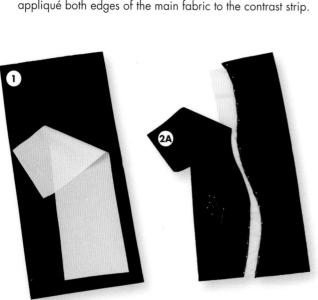

2B For a raw-edged line, cut the main fabric slightly larger than the finished size. Cut a line from contrast fabric and pin or glue-stick it in the center of the main fabric. Topstitch ⅛" (3 mm) from the raw edges of the strip with a short stitch that has good tension. The edges will ravel slightly, giving an organic look, but will hold if your stitching is firm. Remember that wall hangings do not normally get handled and can be a little more fragile than bed quilts.

2C If you prefer, iron fusible web to the back of the contrast fabric before you cut the line; then cut out the line, remove the backing paper, and iron the line to the main fabric. The line will be stiffer than the raw edge one but will not ravel or require topstitching.

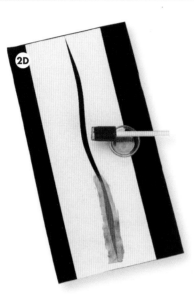

2D Another alternative is to paint the line on the main fabric. Cut a freezer paper strip as long as the fabric and then cut a wavy line in the paper, making it thick and thin. Iron the freezer paper, shiny side down, to the fabric with a dry iron. With a brush or sponge, paint the area between the freezer paper patterns. Peel off the paper, let the paint dry, and then heat set according to the paint manufacturer's directions.

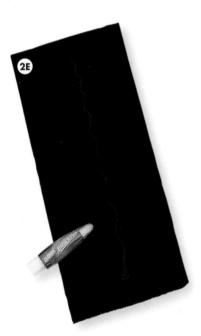

2E Yet another technique for making a line is painting discharge paste or a bleach product onto dark fabric, either freehand or with a freezer paper guide. Process according to the product you've used.

2F Couch yarn down the center of the main fabric, using invisible thread with a zigzag stitch to hold it in place. This might be easier to do after batting has been ironed to the back of the fabric to give it body.

MANY LINES

Make a quilt top with lots of lines and a few feature elements.

1 Cut a variety of fabrics into 1½" to 2" (3.8 to 5.1 cm)-wide strips, remembering to choose fabrics with color and/or value contrast so the separate lines remain distinct. Cut a few strips plus three rectangles of various sizes from your feature fabric(s).

2 Sew enough strips side by side to equal the width of the feature blocks, cut the strip-set into two sections, and add to the tops and bottoms of the blocks. You are the designer, and there are no rules on how you place your strips, how many fabrics make up one strip, etc. The only rules are good composition and workmanship.

3 Place the feature blocks with the strips attached on the design wall. Play with arrangements, thinking about balance and unity, and sew the three sections together. Press well and trim off the top and bottom edges to straighten.

For another look, make lines with screen printing.

1 Make a diagram of various sizes of blocks so they are balanced and interesting. The diagram can be very rough but will save time when cutting out pieces from six different fabrics. Remember to add the seam allowances when you cut the pieces.

2 Arrange the fabric pieces on the design wall and determine the best way to sew them into units with the fewest partial seams. Marking heavy lines along unit divisions on your diagram will help at the sewing machine. Sew the blocks together, pressing the seam allowances open as you go to make them flatter for printing.

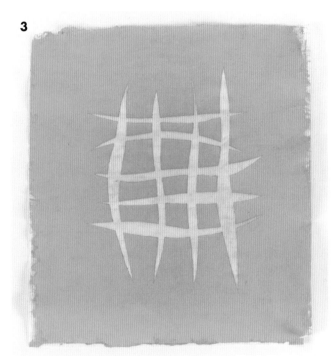

3 Prepare a silk screen with lines by ironing freezer paper shapes to thin interfacing, ironing the interfacing to another sheet of freezer paper, and painting out the background with acrylic paint and/or gesso to seal it. (Use three thin coats.) Pull off the freezer paper lines and back sheet.

4 Place the interfacing on the back of a screen, tape it down, and do some practice runs on newspaper. When the interfacing is saturated with paint, print the design over the quilt top using contrasting colors. Let dry and heat set. (You could also use thickened dye on a light-colored quilt top or discharge products on a dark-colored quilt top, but test all the fabrics first to see that they react the way you expect.)

5 Notice how the printing goes right over the pressed-open seam allowances. The hardest part of printing on a quilt top is knowing when to stop, but generally it is best to print an odd number of motifs.

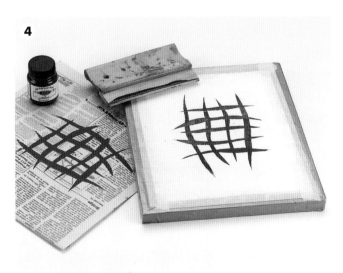

A yard (0.9 m) of hand-dyed or batik striped fabric makes a quick and lovely art quilt, perfect for trying out a new quilting/painting technique later.

1 Fold the stripe in half down the center and then in half again. Cut three piles of 10½" (27 cm) squares through the four layers. Cut the squares diagonally in both directions.

2 Match up similar triangles to make blocks—you will have six that make crosses and six that make squares-in-squares. Sew the triangles together to make blocks. Fabric by Diane Swallen.

Another way to make lines is to choose a light-value hand-dyed fabric and paint it.

1 Tear pieces of masking tape and apply them to the back of a silk screen and squeegee paint through the screen onto the fabric. Let dry and heat set.

2 If the screen starts to clog (a common problem with metallic paint) or you miss a spot, embellish with beads or stitch for the perfect focal point to your art quilt. Remember, exploit your weakness.

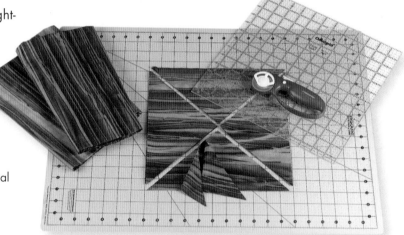

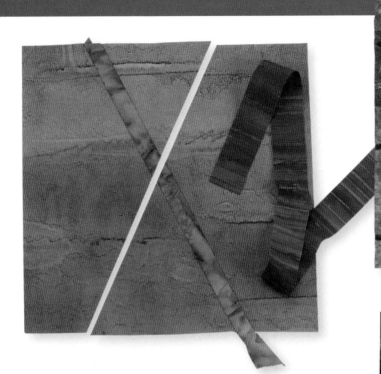

Try this completely different approach.

1 Cut pieces of background fabric(s) into 8½" (21.6 cm) squares. Cut 1" (2.5 cm)- wide strips of various contrasting fabrics. Cut one of the blocks edge to edge with an off-center diagonal line.

2 Piece the two sections of the square onto a strip of fabric. The block should remain the same size as it was, since you are taking out ½" (1.3 cm) in seam allowances and putting it back in with the strip. Press the seam allowances toward the strip to raise it up slightly.

3 Make another cut and piece in another strip of fabric. Cut and piece in one more strip, avoiding cutting through a previous strip intersection.

4 Continue to cut and piece blocks in the same way. If the edges of your blocks are uneven, trim all the blocks down to a uniform size and then piece them together. Overdyed decorator fabric by Wendy Richardson

Expand on the previous idea with a fat quarter or larger piece of fabric. Choose a plain fabric if you want to quilt heavily or a patterned fabric if you don't. Choose a plain contrasting fabric for the lines. Instead of diagonal lines, try straight lines. Be sure to place the piece on the design wall before each cut so balance is maintained and the sections don't get scrambled!

If you like handwork, make a line quilt top with reverse appliqué.

1 Select a fabric with lots of color change!

2 Select a second plain fabric that contrasts with the first, and cut it to the same size. With a chalk pencil, draw lines over the surface of the fabric, leaving a space for a focal point. Pin or baste the two fabrics together.

3 Cut through one of the chalk lines with a scissors, being careful not to cut the bottom fabric. Turn under the raw edges of the cut and hand appliqué them down, making sure the ends of the cut are securely stitched. (Thread is contrasting to show detail.) Continue to cut and stitch all the lines.

4 Create a focal point, either with more reverse appliqué or with a motif added to the top with raw edge or turned-under methods.

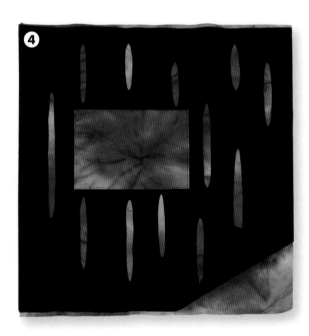

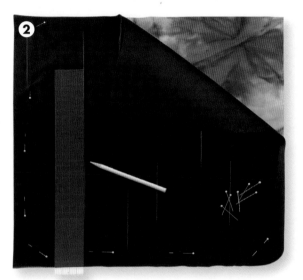

For another effect, cut a commercially printed panel or a small gelatin print like this one by Lucy Senstad into strips and piece in contrasting strips for more interest and complexity. Press the seam allowances away from the inserted strips to maintain the emphasis on the main fabric.

For a background fabric that you would like to expand in size, cut the insert strips wider than ½" (1.3 cm), even going as wide as 3" or 4" (7.6 or 10.2 cm).

A line of a different kind could describe this quilt top. Very simple line drawings, done either with a permanent marker or with the sewing machine, can make a charming wall piece.

1 Iron four different fabrics that coordinate with the background to 8½" x 11" (21.6 x 27.9 cm) sheets of Wonder-Under fusible web. On three pieces, draw four flowers or other images with a black line. On the fourth piece, make an 8" x 10" (20.3 x 25.4 cm) drawing. Peel off the backing paper (using small stitches will help perforate the paper; it isn't necessary to remove every bit of paper except on the edges).

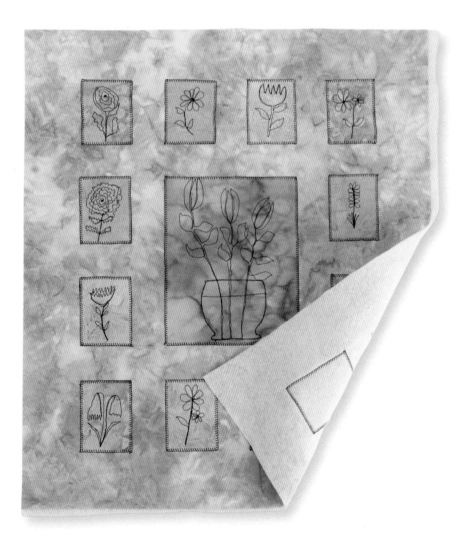

2 Cut a 24½" x 28½" (62.2 x 72.4 cm) background fabric and fuse the drawings onto it, leaving 2" (5.1 cm) spaces between blocks. Hint: press center lines into the background to help place the blocks.

3 Iron the quilt top to fusible batting and use a blanket or other decorative stitch to outline your drawings with black thread.

Generally, black cotton fabrics will react to bleach in any form (bleach pen, liquid, soft cleanser) by turning a reddish brown. Collect some of your discharge samples that have lines in them and collage them together. Back a larger piece with batting and layer the smaller samples on top. Topstitch the edges.

The larger piece by Lucy Senstad is shibori on cotton sateen. The small samples are bleach through zigzag-stitched plastic, sprayed bleach over masking tape resist, sponge-brushed bleach, and sprayed bleach over rug gripper.

Throw caution—or lines—to the wind!

1 Pick a background fabric and then choose contrasting fabrics or one fabric that contains several colors. Cut small pieces of the contrasting fabrics, back them with Wonder-Under fusible web, remove the backing paper, and cut them into strips. Cut the strips into shorter pieces.

2 Place the little pieces over the surface of the background, making sure the fusible web is down. Iron over the pieces to fuse them, using a piece of cooking parchment to protect the iron—just in case.

Landscapes

Most of us enjoy a certain kind of landscape—mountains, desert, ocean, or woods. Some of us love all of them.

Putting what you love into your art quilts is very satisfying and does not have to be difficult. The viewer will know what you are portraying by reading color and/or shape, even if your mountain is chartreuse or your tree is a triangle on a stick. Landscape quilts allow you to use every technique in your toolbox and be subtle or outrageous. Keep in mind that most of these landscapes are unfinished and will have stitching and/or quilting added for detail and texture.

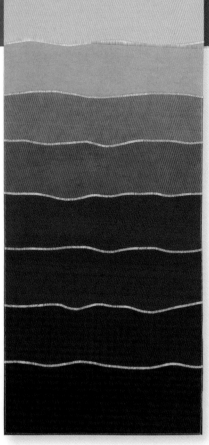

A sun-dappled woods is portrayed with a hand-dyed piece of striped fabric with defined trees represented by strips of textured gray fabric. The photo of the young blue jay is printed on T-shirt transfer paper for dark fabrics and ironed onto the background according to package directions. When it comes time to stitch and quilt the piece, bark can be added to the trees if desired. Striped fabric by Diane Swallen.

A little less abstract, this landscape uses hand-dyed fabrics with pattern and texture. The hills are turned-under appliqué done with a blind-hem stitch and invisible thread. A fused tree is added for a focal point. The appliqué and quilting are accomplished in the same operation but, of course, a lot more quilting could be added for interest and texture.

For a simple yet dramatic abstract landscape, choose a bundle of eight hand-dyed fat quarters or eight scrap pieces from your stash. Cut a piece of fusible batting about 14" x 30" (35.6 x 76.2 cm). Cut a piece from each fabric about 5" x 12" (12.7 x 30.5 cm), and cut a curved edge on one side. Iron the pieces to the batting, overlapping an inch or two (2.5 or 5 cm). Pin the curved edges and satin-stitch them with light-colored thread. Add a narrow border or trim off the excess batting and back/bind. Fabric by Cherrywood Fabrics.

CURVY HILLS

1 To begin a landscape like this, cut a piece of fusible batting and fuse on the top piece of fabric with a steam iron.

2 Cut a second hill with curves on the top edge, iron under the seam allowance on the top, pin it down over the first piece, and blind-hem the edge with invisible thread.

3 Add embroidered plants to the hills for texture and interest.

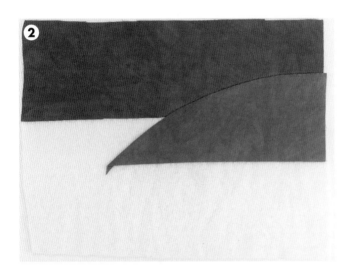

STRAIGHT EDGES

A variation is the straight-edged landscape.

1 Cut strips of fabric at a slight angle and sew to the batting with a walking foot, right sides together. Iron each strip over onto the fusible batting as you sew.

2 When the strips are completed, add borders if desired and then add mini-elements like small appliquéd or photo-transferred images to complement and contrast with the strip fabrics.

3 Use prepared bias tape to cover the edges of the elements and topstitch them on top of the quilt.

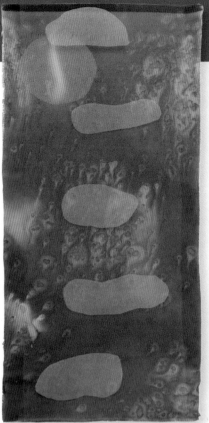
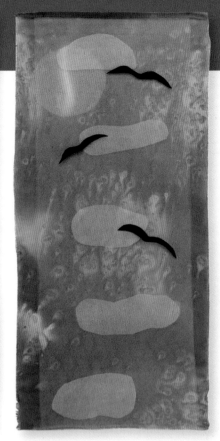

SHEER OVERLAY

1 Tear or cut a piece of painted blue silk. Hem the edges if they are cut, and fuse a yellow sun onto the blue silk with Mistyfuse or Wonder-Under.

2 Cut two pieces of white netting narrower than the silk, and fuse white silk on one piece for clouds and black bird silhouettes on the top piece. Hint: Using netting on a roll saves cutting the side edges and the edges won't ravel.

3 Turn the silk down over the two netting pieces, and hem the top edges together.

If you are lucky enough to find an ombre sheer, you can make a simple but complex-looking little landscape. Cut a section of "sky" color and pin it to white fabric. Cut a wide strip of sheer and back it with Mistyfuse. With a rotary cutter, make curvy slices from the hombre sheer, overlap the slices on the white fabric, and fuse. Be sure to turn the iron down if the sheer is nylon.

This little piece is based on a painted fabric by Mickey Lawler and incorporates netting, cheesecloth, and scrim to suggest clouds and water.

Create an abstract landscape with the qualities of stained glass.

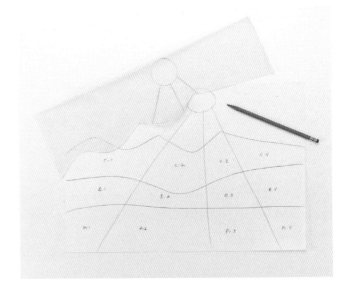

1 Draw a simple pattern the size of the finished wall hanging. Divide the scene with diagonal lines. Make a tracing of the pattern and number the parts on both copies. Cut the tracing apart along the horizontal lines.

2 Cut a piece of black fabric the size of the drawing plus ¼" (6 mm) seam allowances, and cover with black Mistyfuse web, using a piece of baking parchment to protect the iron.

3 Cut the sky piece with the pattern, trimming a scant ⅛" (3 mm) off the curved edge as you cut and adding ¼" (6 mm) on the top and side edges. Fuse the sky to the black fabric, being careful not to touch the iron to the exposed fusible web.

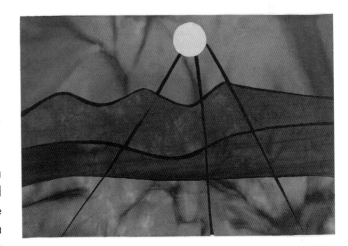

4 Cut the land shapes and slice them along the diagonal lines, trimming off a scant ⅛" (3 mm) on all interior cuts and adding ¼" (6 mm) to the exterior edges. Fuse everything to the black fabric.

5 Add the sun and rays to the sky. (Trimming the ⅛" [3 mm] irregularly makes the separations more interesting.) Fabrics by Diane Bartels.

Landscapes done with texture can range from undersea scenes to beach settings to mountain vistas. Think of all the materials you may have that suggest elements like sand, rocks, fences, and clouds. Pull out the Angelina fibers to add glisten to water or melt Tyvek to make a rocky shore. The sky is the limit when you are creating landscapes—even rocks can be glued to the surface as long as the quilt is heavy enough to support them.

These samples are just the simplest of ideas for landscape quilts. Depending on your interests, you can create very detailed and realistic scenes with fusing or appliqué, panoramas that you paint on cloth and then stitch, or photo transfers that you alter in the computer and print onto fabric. Your vistas are unlimited!

Create a patchwork background (this one is a log cabin, with the light values making mountains) and fuse an abstract landscape element over it.

Texture

There are two kinds of textures—visual and tactile. Many art quilters use both types, with or without recognizable images, to invite the viewer in for a closer look.

Since surface design is a huge focus in the last two decades, dyeing, painting, discharging color, and fabric manipulation all present many choices for a new piece. Either purchased or created in your own studio, cloth with texture is irresistible.

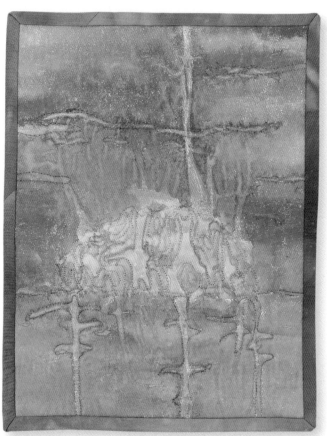

A second piece by Sue shows painted Wonder-Under used as the entire background with stitching following the striations in the painted web. 81/2" x 11" (21.5 x 28 cm)

This piece by Sue Kelly shows wonderful texture both in the circles created with painted Wonder-Under and in the stitching done with cotton and metallic threads. 8½" x 11" (21.5 x 28 cm)

PAINTING WONDER-UNDER

1 Use Dye-na-Flow or diluted Lumiere paints to quickly cover the adhesive side of the fusible web, using as many colors as you like.

2 After the backing paper is completely dry, use it whole or cut a motif and turn it adhesive-side down on a piece of fabric and iron to transfer the web. After the web is on the fabric, cover it with a clean piece of baking parchment and iron again to firmly attach all the adhesive.

To create a thread feature like Sue's below:

1 Cut lots of threads and gather them together on a piece of Sulky Solvy. Include little scraps of lamé if you like.

2 Cover with another piece of Solvy and stitch a grid over the top. Be sure to catch all the threads inside.

3 Dissolve the Solvy by soaking in warm water for 15 minutes and then rinsing to remove all sticky stabilizer.

4 Stitch the thread element to the background.

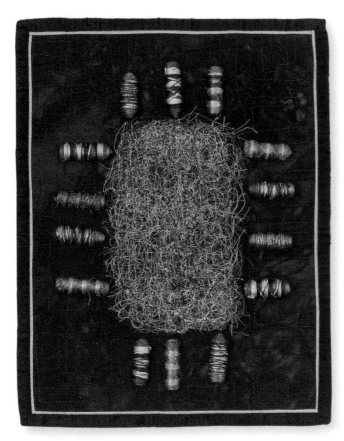

A lot of texture packed into a little piece, this one features metallic threads stitched between layers of Sulky Solvy and large beads made from Tyvek and wrapped with thread and embroidery floss. Notice the tiny piped edge made from gold lamé and textured silk dupioni on the binding. Made by Sue Kelly. 8½" x 11" (21.5 x 28 cm)

SILK CARRIER RODS

Silk carrier rods are rough, ugly little strips that are left after a cocoon is unreeled by machine. After a bath in Dye-na-Flow, however, they are great textural elements in a small wall piece.

1 Pour some paint into a cup and soak the rods for a few minutes. Dry on a paper towel and then iron to flatten.

2 Sew the painted rods to a colorful piece of commercially hand-dyed fabric using metallic thread and embellish with felted trim.

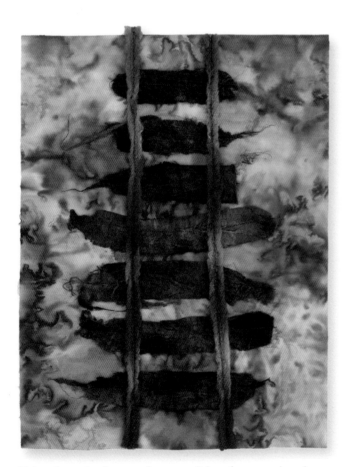

This piece is the perfect candidate for some hand beading for even more texture.

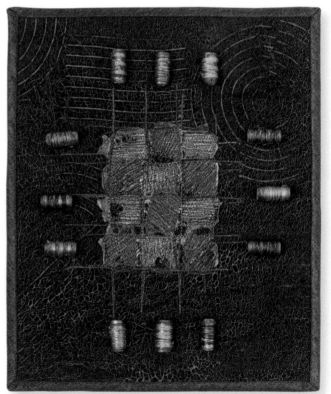

Sue Kelly again combines great texture and stitch. Melted and painted Tyvek is heavily covered with stitching, leaving only tiny curled edges exposed. Couched threads run across the Tyvek grid and onto the discharged background fabric. Tyvek beads add dimension. 10" x 12" (25.4 x 30.5 cm)

MELTING TYVEK

1 Place the Tyvek on an ironing surface in a well-ventilated area and hold a hot iron just above the surface until it distorts. Holding the iron on each side will create different patterns.

2 Paint the Tyvek with Lumiere and cut out motifs. Or stitch a grid on the Tyvek and then distort and paint it.

3 Cut leaves out of the painted Tyvek sheet and stitch them with veins to attach them to the quilt.

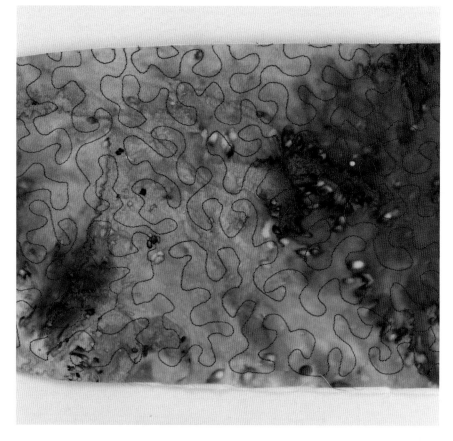

TEXTURE MAGIC

Texture Magic by Superior makes texturing fabric quick and easy.

1 Sew the Texture Magic to the back of the fabric with lots of stitching.

2 Hold the steam iron over the back to shrink the material.

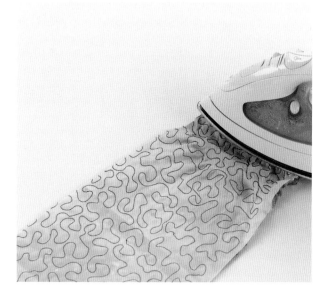

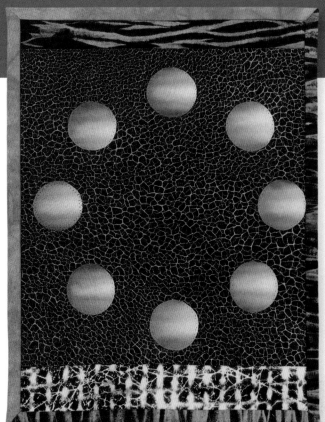

Sue Kelly's quilt is discharged using potato dextrin as a resist. Two other pieces of discharged fabric add interest and simple blue circles add all the detail needed for this wonderful composition. Notice how blue is used for half of the binding to echo the circle color. 8½" x 11" (21.5 x 28 cm)

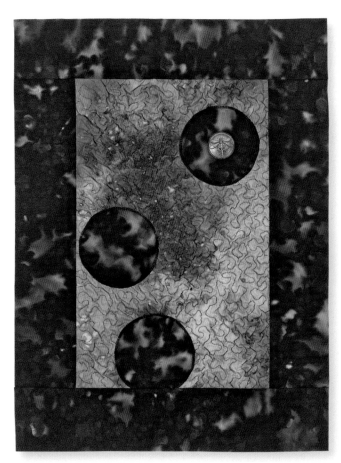

To highlight a great glass button, texture a back-ground, sew on large circles, and place the button in the center of one.

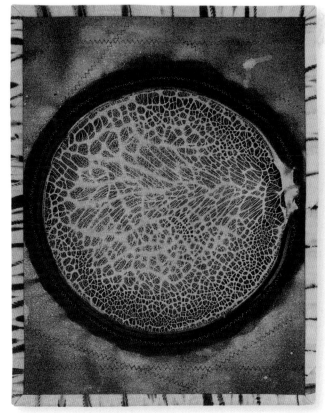

Sue used potato dextrin discharge for this piece as well but added nothing to the dramatic surface design except zigzag quilting in metallic thread. 8½" x 11" (21.5 x 28 cm)

Photographs of outdoor features can be great starting places for textural treatments, either visual or tactile. Use your camera to record the details in the scenery you enjoy—and you'll have a rich resource for those long winter months.

For a completely different look, add Angelina and foil to your next art quilt. Sue Kelly is a master at using Angelina—keeping it shiny, integrating it into the overall design, and stitching over it to add even more texture.

This photo of the bottom of a pool in Yellowstone National Park could be used as a photo transfer onto fabric, as a sheer organza overlay over neutral fabric, or as dyed cheesecloth built up to represent the mineral deposits. Another approach might be to use puff paint to imitate the ridges.

This peacock feather quilt is stunning in its elegance and simplicity, incorporating stitch brilliantly. Angelina shreds are used for the feather and Bo-Nash 007 bonding powder adheres foil to the background. 8½" x 11" (21.5 x 28 cm)

Here the photo has been printed onto ExtravOrganza sheer fabric and adhered with Mistyfuse. The background fabric was painted by layering silk, cotton, and cheesecloth and pouring diluted paint on top of the layers. When the paint dried, the layers were peeled apart to reveal the cotton with imprints from the cheesecloth. Sometimes the best painting is the kind you don't control at all! The photo doesn't stand out from the background but integrates with it, both in texture and in color. The next step in the development of this art quilt is topstitching.

To foil using bonding powder:

1 Sprinkle the granules over the surface of the fabric.

2 Cover the surface with baking parchment and iron the granules into the fabric.

3 Lay a piece of foil over the fabric, color side up, and burnish the foil sheet with the edge of an iron. The foil will transfer wherever there is adhesive.

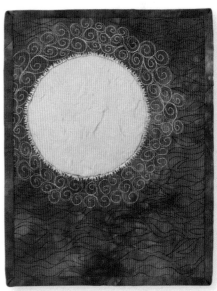

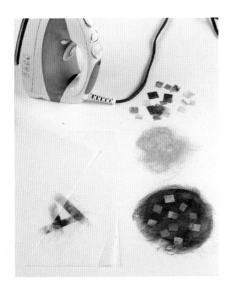

To make an Angelina appliqué:

1 Place shreds between two layers of baking parchment and iron over the top for two or three seconds. Check to see if the shreds are fused together, and iron again if they are not. If the shreds change color, lower the temperature on the iron.

2 Sew, glue, or trap the appliqué under netting to attach it to the fabric background.

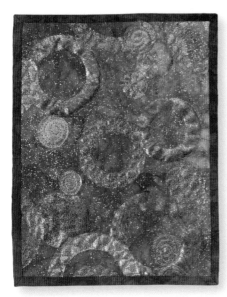

This Sue Kelly quilt features both foil rings, circles, and sprinkles and Angelina appliqués plus lots of free-motion stitching. 8½" x 11" (21.5 x 28 cm)

Heating synthetic fabrics can make interesting texture. A heat gun used for embossing works well—make sure your work area is well-ventilated. After the fabric is shrunk, you can bead into the depressions or just stitch over or around it. This is a polyester curtain fabric.

Sue added lots of stitching around this lovely piece of altered synthetic, which served to flatten the background and raise the sphere higher. 8½" x 11" (21.5 x 28 cm)

Layers

Layering of sheer fabrics, paper, cheesecloth, and tulle is very popular and great fun, especially since many of us "need" to go out and purchase different materials from what is in our stashes.

The layers can be held together with stitching, adhesive, or fusible web, and which one is chosen depends partly on what you want the final project to feel like. Adhesives will make things quite stiff, although a textile medium will be softer than acrylic medium or white glue. Fusible web also makes the quilt stiff generally, but newer products like Mistyfuse are much softer than anything we've used in the past. Stitching by itself creates added texture without stiffness and pulls the layers together so the underneath layers become more visible. While all three methods create tactile texture, depending on the materials used, stitches do what no adhesive or fusible can do: rise off the surface and make a secondary design, while also creating little hills and valleys between lines of stitching. Stitching can be combined with adhesives and fusibles but will not have the same texturing effect of puffing up the in-between areas. Play with several approaches and decide for yourself what you like best.

A piece of fabric weaving that was already quilted was the starting point for this piece. A batik mask fabric was placed on top (a few granules of Bo-Nash 007 bonding powder will hold a layer in place without stiffening it) and then a layer of black net with metallic lines through it was laid over the entire surface. Stitching was done around the mask panel but no other quilting was done over the mask, to keep the layers more fluid. Finally, pieces of colorful knitting tape were stitched down the centers to keep them dimensional. Be aware that when you use anything metallic, it will catch the light and be very dominant. 12" x 18" (30.5 x 46 cm)

Starting with a bold black-and-white print fabric makes an interesting base for a layered piece. Photo transfers on organza, hand-dyed sheers, and hand-dyed rickrack were laid on top of the print fabric and then a very thin head scarf, the kind you used to buy at the dime store, was added to capture all the small pieces. After pinning everything down, a grid was stitched over the whole piece. 18" x 12" (46 x 30.5 cm)

A beautiful piece of silk organza can act as a fluttery layer over an art quilt that has high contrast and will be transparent. Bind the quilt on the bottom and sides and include the hemmed (or not) organza layer in the top binding. For a pictorial quilt like this, print the photos on opaque cotton inkjet sheets instead of sheer organza. Organza overlay by Wendy Richardson. 14" x 21½" (35.5 x 54.5 cm)

A piece of overdyed decorator fabric and two photo transfers on organza covered by hand-dyed organza are the basis for this layered piece. Ribbon, a button, and lace add surface accents and stitching follows the lines in the fabrics. Satin stitching was used to bring out a metal trellis in one of the photos. Fabrics by Wendy Richardson. 33½" x 11" (85 x 28 cm)

Paper/cloth lamination is definitely a layering process and can include a large variety of materials, due to the adhesive qualities of the fluid acrylic medium. Sheer papers and fabrics, ribbons, photo transfers on organza, and cheesecloth all work well. Start with a piece of freezer paper coated with medium and build until you're satisfied, adding medium along the way to make sure everything is firmly attached. Stitching can be added once everything is dry. 16" x 20" (40.5 x 51 cm)

Use netting instead of organza if you prefer the under layers to show more. This sample shows a needle-punched flower that is partially covered with black netting and then punched from the back to bring the wool roving up through the net. Ribbons layered over the netting secure it and add texture and interest.

Print a favorite poem or quote on an ExtravOrganza inkjet fabric sheet. Peel the fabric off the backing fabric, keeping the grain of the fabric as straight as possible, and place a piece of Mistyfuse web on the back side. Cover with baking parchment and lightly press with a dry iron so the web sticks to the organza. Print a photo on inkjet cotton, peel off the backing paper, and fuse the organza over it. Embellish if you like and, of course, the stitching is still to come.

Choose cotton, linen, rayon, or silk fabrics for bottom layers and a synthetic sheer for the top layer(s) to make a distressed piece.

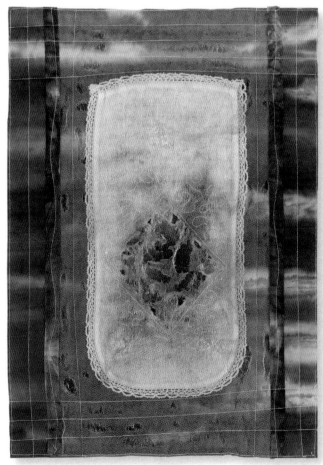

Here a vintage linen arm cover has been dye-painted and sewn to a base fabric and batting (cotton/poly). Nylon netting is stitched over the layers with cotton thread (the density of the stitching will affect the amount of melting) and then melted with a heat gun. A worn old piece has been rescued and renewed for many more years of enjoyment. Linen dyed by Wendy Richardson.

Layering with painted Wonder-Under is always fun and unpredictable.

1 Tape a piece of Wonder-Under to your painting surface and stamp an opaque paint onto the rough side with a large foam stamp. Let dry.

2 Cover the whole surface with Dye-na-Flow paint and let dry.

3 Iron the painted side of the Wonder-Under onto a piece of fabric and carefully peel off the release paper (some of the web may not transfer). Place a clean piece of baking parchment over the fabric and press again.

4 Embellish the fabric with fabric cutouts or a sheer layer of netting or cheesecloth by laying them down, covering with baking parchment, and pressing. Trap ribbons or cutouts under the netting if you wish. The fusible web may be slightly sticky to begin with, but by the time you quilt, there will be no problem. Remember to always protect the web with parchment when ironing.

Paint four squares of Lutradur with four different colors of diluted Dye-na-Flow paint and let dry. Stack the pieces and stitch around the edges to hold them together. Using a heat gun, melt down through the layers to reveal the different colors. Stitch the square into a small quilt and use variegated thread to quilt. A metal washer painted with alcohol ink adds the finishing touch.

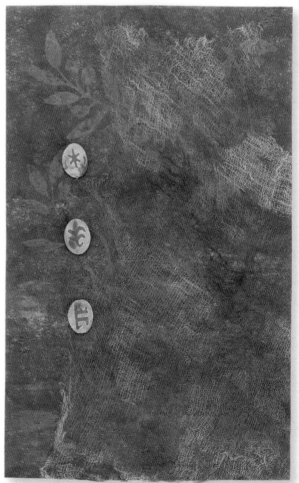

PAINTED LAYERS

Other kinds of layers that depend less on fabric choices and more on surface design are also popular among art quilters and mixed-media enthusiasts. Printing allows the layering of transparent paint or dye using screens and stamps. Digital techniques let you layer images on the computer and print out finished montages. Painting, dyeing, and discharging using resists and reductive processes open up all kinds of possibilities.

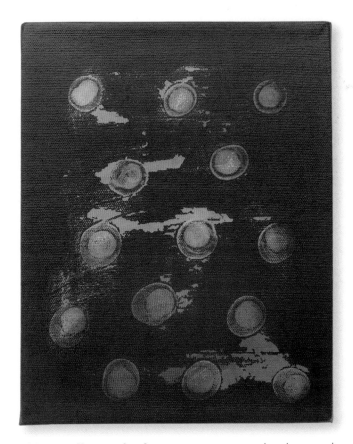

Kit Eastman is a master at creating mystery and complexity with printing. Her quilt "Gathering" is a wonderful representation of autumn. 43" x 17" (109 x 43 cm). Be sure to visit her website to see many more examples of her work. www.kiteastman.com

This small stretched canvas was painted with several colors of acrylic paint and allowed to dry. It was then painted with diluted black acrylic, and a bleach pen was used to draw circles into the wet paint. The bleach was left to dry overnight and then scrubbed off with water and a toothbrush, revealing the colors underneath. Spray fixative stabilizes the surface.

Text

You will find words appearing on art quilts of all sizes and styles. Some are running commentaries that fill every open space on the quilt top; others are headlines making a statement; and others are poetry or phrases that fit the theme of the quilt. Still other uses of text say nothing but add a dynamic visual element.

Text can be applied to the quilt top in many ways, including surface design and stitching. Choose what you wish to say and dive in.

Rubber stamps seem to collect in our studios and are a fun and easy way to begin a quilt top. Choose statements about art, if you like, as in this sample. Stamping onto a small piece of contrasting fabric that is added to a background ensures you won't mess up the whole piece if an image smears or is faint; this technique also highlights the quote.

Adding text to a patchwork quilt top is actually not new—in times of war, quilt tops were circulated by Red Cross workers to collect money, and donors had their names printed on a patch.

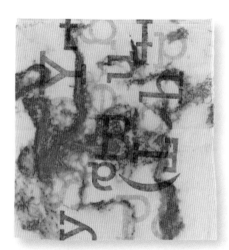

Wendy Richardson uses text to tie elements together in this wonderful piece of vintage ribbon. Different stamped images overlap and the text areas carry the eye and add texture, even if the viewer can't read some of the words.

If you have access to an old letter press, arrange letters and make a print. The background fabric here was rusted for lots of texture and a feeling of age.

Here a wild log cabin touts its colors by listing different names of red in the strips. Individual letter stamps were used, giving the words a quirky look and surrounding them with black smudges from the stamp.

Sun print using Dye-na-Flow paint and a cutout paper stencil from the scrapbooking store. Starting with a light-colored batik, this sample was sprayed with water and then painted all over with paint. The stencil was placed on top, and the fabric was put out in hot sun to dry. The print developed during the drying process and then was ironed to set it permanently. Use the fabric as a background for a collage, or stitch into some of the letters with hand embroidery.

A gelatin print made by Lucy Senstad was embellished with text by stenciling with a Paintstik. Stencils are a great way to add words without practicing your calligraphy! Paintstik color will work on any fiber and is permanent after heat setting.

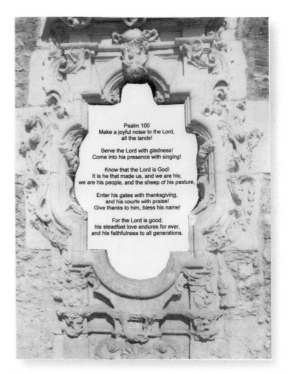

Collect fabrics like this overdyed decorator print with text on it, a sheer silk piece, three little overdyed botanical prints, a piece of embroidered ribbon, and an abstract leaf screen print. The pieces are tied together by color as well as the emphasis on line, subject, and words. Place the elements on the design wall and play with different arrangements. To fill in an open area, print a poem on ExtravOrganza and stitch that over the background, letting the text on the original fabric show through. Fabrics by Rosemary Kessler, Diane Bartels, Wendy Richardson.

If you have a photo of a window or door, like this one from an old mission in San Antonio, use it as a frame for a favorite verse. Print the photo onto transfer paper and the verse onto inkjet cotton. Cut out the space within the window frame and press the transfer paper onto the cotton, framing the verse. Remember that the window frame will be reversed when ironed to the cotton.

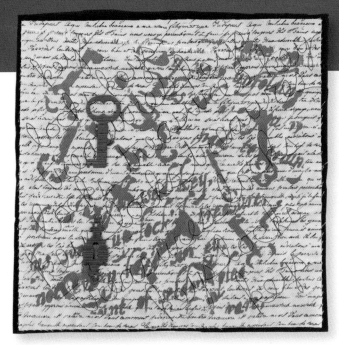

Layer as many kinds of text as you like, since it's not the actual words that matter, but the texture and line. Here a commercial print with foreign words on it is stenciled with keys and words relating to them, and then free-motion stitching goes over the top. Lumiere paint is used for both the stenciling and to color two grungeboard shapes (scrapbook or craft store),which are glued on after quilting and provide the focal point for the quilt. Stencil by www.TheCraftersWorkshop.com.

Feel strongly about something? Make a statement by creating a rubbing plate from graph paper and stickers. Spell out a word or phrase and stick the letters to the paper. Place the paper on a nonslip surface, or tape it to the table and place a piece of fabric over it. With the peeled side of a Paintstik, carefully rub over the letters. Move the fabric and repeat the rubbing as many times as you like, being careful not to smear previous painting. Let the paint dry for two or three days, heat set with an iron, and finish your art quilt.

Screen printing is the easiest way to print text over and over to make a complex and textured fabric. A simple temporary screen can be made by using a soldering iron to cut a Tyvek stencil, which is then taped to a blank screen. Print the text as many times as you like and then clean and remove the stencil for future use. For script writing, try to avoid closed loops if you want the text to be legible; for an abstract look, it doesn't matter.

Make a special greeting or gift by applying resist to fabric and doing a wash of diluted Dye-na-Flow over it. Use Elmer's School Glue, soy wax, or water-soluble gutta to write a message and decorate white fabric, making sure the resist goes all the way through to the back. Let the resist dry thoroughly, and then spray the fabric with water and paint over the entire surface. After the paint is dry, iron it to set the color, and then soak out the resist in hot water. (If using soy wax, place the fabric on newsprint when you heat set it, removing most of the wax at the same time.) Here a bit of foil was added for even more excitement!

Mother's arms are made of tenderness & sweet sleep blesses the child who lies therein. VICTOR HUGO

Gina Sekelsky is a master calligrapher who wrote out this quote with a Paintstik, having never used one before! Place your fabric on a nonslip surface to write, let the paint dry for two or three days, and then iron to make the paint permanent. http://richinnerlife.typepad.com.

Bleach pens are the perfect way to discharge black cotton or rayon fabric with words. Simply write with the pen and wait for the color to change. Rinse the fabric in soapy water and then soak it in a neutralizing solution of Anti-Chlor and water. Rinse again. Sun printed fabric by Diane Bartels.

Having a Thermofax screen made will provide a very clear and durable way to print text onto fabric. Make sure the scale of the text relates to the size of the art quilt. If you overlap printings, wipe the back of the screen between prints so you don't transfer ghost images.

Collect headlines from magazines and newspapers or create your own on the computer, tape them to copy paper, and then copy them onto prepared inkjet cotton sheets. Cut apart and make a collage. This one includes odds and ends like a silk painting sample, a stamped quote, and a fish rubbing. The headlines convey the ways art impacts a life—from exploration of new techniques, to traveling to quilt shows and classes, to therapy for a long, dreary winter. The background is simply written on with a permanent marker to suggest the theme of the quilt.

People and Faces

It's always fun to portray people in quilts, with all our idiosyncrasies, expressions, and activities. It is also intimidating, because a face can be pretty grotesque if done badly.

Fortunately, there are many different ways to produce faces with a minimum of lines and features and without taking a life drawing class. Just as with landscapes, the eye knows what it is seeing with just a few clues. Have fun creating a cast of characters after looking at the samples in this chapter and then make up some entirely new ways to populate your art quilts.

Start with stick figures. The arms and legs can be drawn onto the fabric with marker, embroidered by hand, painted with a fine brush, or even drawn on the computer and printed out. Dress your figure simply and add a button or circle of fabric for a face. Place your figure on a background that tells a story. Background fabric by Mickey Lawler, www.skydyes.com.

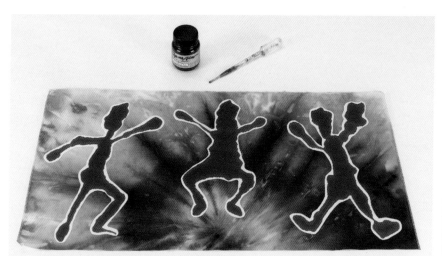

The Dribble People might be the name for this piece. Dye-na-Flow paint was drawn onto white fabric with a pipette. The paint flowed freely until whimsical figures appeared. After drying and heat setting, the figures were cut out and fused to a background. This would serve as a great background for text or an opportunity to go crazy with beading.

Take stick figures a step further with fused sticks. Back some brown fabric with fusible web, peel the backing paper off, and then cut freehand sticks. Fuse them to a background and then dress the figure with yarn or fabric.

Simple modified rectangles can become abstract people with an ethnic flair. Choose fabrics that represent Africa, South America, or the Southwest United States and cut rectangles with rounded tops. Draw simple head shapes and embellish with feathers, hats, or bands and then fuse or appliqué everything to a background. Add necklaces if you like. You could also make the clothing with strip piecing, embroidery, or collage. Add a pieced border with an ethnic feel.

For a slightly more realistic quilt, without faces at all, show the backs of a row of people with more curved lines and posture showing. Add more details in the clothing with stitching or paint if you wish. The head bands can be dimensional on a larger piece, attached only at the ends. Black satin stitching separates the figures and finishes the edges.

Create simple figures with featureless faces. On a simple landscape background, layer faces, hair, and clothing that are abstract but interesting in texture. The viewer's eye will read the shapes as figures and their minds will add the story.

The next step is drawing faces—a challenge for some of us! The following samples are inspired by quilts in magazines and books.

1 This singer has a fused mouth with painted teeth and nose and eyes drawn with marker. Embroidery could be used instead. Hair could be yarn, stitching, or fused fabric in the shape of a hat or strings of hair.

2 One way to avoid drawing eyes is to use sunglasses instead.

3 For that vacant stare look, use white lenses!

4 Some artists divide the face in half and ignore reality completely!

Sue Kelly uses the divided face idea much more realistically in this sample, illustrating a quote from the novel *Loud and Clear* by Anna Quindlen: "Afterward my head looked perpetually surprised."

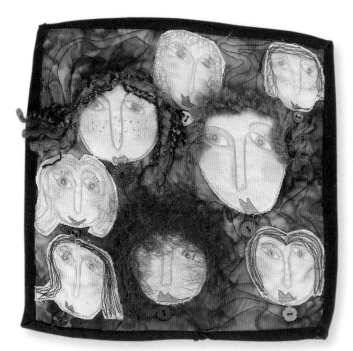

For super-realistic faces, try photo transfer. Use photo transfer paper to print the face onto any fabric. Just remember that the image will be reversed. Bring up a face on the computer, enlarge it to 8" x 10" (20.3 x 25.4), remove the paper from the feed tray of the printer, and insert one sheet of photo transfer paper. Print and then iron the print to the fabric with a dry iron, following manufacturer's directions.

Nancy Hoerner has a great way to make faces that are fun and lively—she draws them without looking! Draw on fabric with a pencil while looking somewhere else and then highlight the lines with colored pencils and stitching. Add details with colored pencils and Paintstiks, and then cut the faces out and sew to a background, adding funky hair and buttons for embellishments.

This portrait could be called "His Head Is in the Clouds" or "Airhead!"

A funny photo is altered with a special-effects filter (poster edges) in Photoshop and printed onto prepared inkjet cotton. Use the photo as a focal point for a collage or as part of a collection of "dogs I have known" pieces.

Sue Kelly's answer to a self-portrait challenge was to show herself behind her camera. The monochromatic color scheme makes the piece very dramatic. 21" x 26" (53.5 x 66 cm)

Maria Elkins is a master quilt portrait artist who teaches in person and on a DVD called *Making Faces,* available from Interweave Press. "Violinist" is a portrait of her daughter that highlights the passion of Lydia's playing and the light bouncing off her hair. It is all fused appliqué using various brown fabrics, with lovely quilting to impart texture and movement. Check out Maria's website at www.mariaelkins.com.

Maria's 17" (43 cm) square piece called "Sheer Whim" is an extremely engaging portrait employing black fabric, Paintstik and ink texturing, and netting overlays. Beautiful feather quilting adds a secondary pattern over the portrait. You could look into those eyes forever.

Doroth Mayer uses cyanotype processes to transfer images to cloth, which involves using photographic chemicals, negatives, and exposure to the sun to print both brown and blue photos. This piece includes antique photos of family and a picture of Doroth while undergoing treatment for breast cancer. Goddess images are painted and beaded onto a rusted fabric and silk matka lends a contrast in texture. 21" x 26" (53.5 x 66 cm)

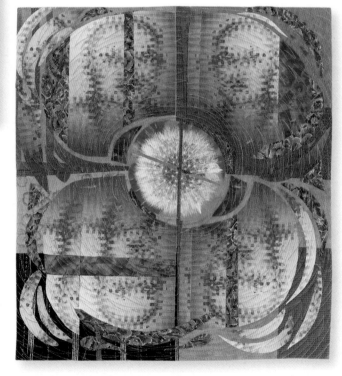

Doroth made this piece also during breast cancer treatment. The puff ball and four fractured images of her face represent the way that she felt her brain operated during that very difficult period. Elements were fused to a pieced background of silk and cotton. Stitching unifies the piece and adds to the frazzled look. 21½" x 26" (53.5 x 66 cm)

Finally, what would a chapter about putting people on quilts be without a couple of pets? Barbara Matthiessen created a tribute to Daisy the cat with appliqué and stitching. Notice the machine-programmed stitching around the face with Daisy's name and date.

Scotty's name is boldly appliquéd and stitched alongside Barbara's dog portrait. Thread painting lends texture and shading to the picture, and the black-and-white binding adds a sense of fun.

Flowers

Flowers are the universally popular subject for all quilters—traditional, transitional, or contemporary. Once again, an abstract shape put into the right context will read as a flower. Or the flower can be very literal.

Use photo transfer paper to make a garden of images. Choose related photos or create a garden with a profusion of various blooms.

You can also use a marker to stencil designs over the photo. Another alternative is using a wet cotton swab to push the ink around on the transfer paper and then let it dry before ironing. The semitransparent quality of the photo transfer paper image allows the background fabric to show through, altering the colors and integrating the photos at the same time.

To print with photo transfer paper:

1 Bring an image up on the computer and adjust the print settings for letter size and fit to page, which gives you a slightly larger image than selecting the standard 8" x 10" (20.3 x 25.4 cm) photo size. Place the photo transfer paper in the paper tray of the printer by itself, making sure the white side is the one that will be printed on. Print.

2 Distress the image with a toothpick, if desired.

3 Trim off the white edges around the image. Turn the photo right side down on fabric and iron with a dry iron over the back of the transfer paper, moving the iron constantly and making sure the edges are firmly adhered. The backing paper should peel off easily when the image is transferred—keep checking a corner until that happens.

4 Potential problems may occur when ironing is uneven, leaving some ink on the backing paper; when the iron is too hot, resulting in curling of the fabric; or when the backing paper is not peeled in one smooth operation, resulting in a line of ink at the hesitation point.

This fun and easy flower quilt that was made by Susan Antell (in a class taught by Laura Wasilowski, who also dyed the fabric) started with bright rainbow-colored hand-dyed fabric. Susan ironed Wonder-Under to the back of the multicolored fabric using a dry iron. The backing paper was peeled off and simple petals and flower shapes were cut. Leaves were cut with a special rotary cutter blade and the pieces were fused together. Machine stitching and hand embroidery with perle cotton add wonderful texture and detail. 14" x 12½" (35.5 x 32 cm)

Here the focus image is ironed onto white fabric and then bordered for emphasis, while the other images are distressed with a toothpick while still on the transfer paper and then ironed onto the painted background (Mickey Lawler, www.skydyes.com).

Doroth uses the tiling method of transferring a photo to fabric, which means dividing an image into smaller units, printing them, and then sewing them back together to form the entire picture. Rather than sewing the tiles together to cover up the joins, Doroth adds contrasting strips between them. Hand-dyed greens extend the leaves from the photo into the border, which is emphasized with stitching. Beading adds sparkle, dimension, and interest to the flower centers. This quilt was made following Doroth's successful battle with breast cancer. 22" x 26½" (56 x 67.5 cm)

Doroth Mayer uses photographic negatives with cyanotype processes to make blue or brown images on fabric. This piece uses photos of structures, flowers, and lace printed onto fabric and complements them with old linens dyed to match, which also feature flower images. A few textured fabrics in different colors accent the blue, and metallic stitching, beading, stamping, and embellishments add wonderful detail. The viewer has a lot to look at and enjoy in this delicate quilt. 23" x 23" (58.5 x 58.5 cm)

A simple yet effective flower quilt can be made with a brooch purchased from a favorite artist. Eve Brown makes wonderful distressed fabric flowers by melting circles of hand-dyed cloth until they curl up and develop wavy edges. A pin back makes it easy to attach the flower to the raw-edge background. Background fabric by Diane Swallen, Diane Bartels, and Wendy Richardson.

Sometimes fabric needs very little to make it shine. A large commercial rose print combined with a discharged black fabric with the bleached-out dots recolored in red and gold by Diane Bartels makes a dynamic floral quilt. Stitching will be all that is needed to complete it.

Painting flowers is quick and easy and ensures results that are truly one of a kind. Cut off the end of a stalk of celery for a perfect rose stamp! With a sponge, load the cut end with opaque fabric paint and stamp onto fabric. If painting on white fabric, let the paint dry and then do a wash with diluted Dye-na-Flow for a pretty background. After the paint is dry, iron to set it.

Paint flowers with a stencil, opaque fabric paint, and a sponge dauber. Starting with a leafy batik gives you a ready-made background for lots of blooms.

A stencil may be used a different way for a more delicate look. Smear Paintstik around the opening in the stencil and then brush into the opening with a stencil brush for a soft, shaded effect. To create a pretty fence for your flowers to grow on, place a piece of embossed wallpaper underneath the fabric and use the side of a paintstik to make a rubbing. Let the paint dry for two days, and then iron to set. Stencil by www.LauraMurrayDesigns.com; dyed fabric by Diane Swallen.

Paint twill or habotai silk with diluted Dye-na-Flow. Sprinkle with coarse salt while it is wet if you want lots of texture. After the silk dries, iron it to set the color. Cut petals freehand (larger than the finished size) and hold them in the side of a candle flame to singe the edges, which prevents raveling and creates a nice gray edge. Pull off the charred bits and topstitch onto a background.

Say it all. Show a detailed version of a thistle with a stamped image, fuse on some simple thistle shapes, and make a statement with a text stamp. Simple pieces like this require a good choice of background and good composition (unity, balance, and movement).

Little snippets of brightly colored fabric can make a fun garden scene. With a rotary cutter, make confetti and sprinkle it onto a piece of Sulky Solvy water-soluble stabilizer. Cover with another piece of Solvy and stitch all over the surface, making sure you catch all the little pieces. Soak the sewn piece in warm water and rinse until the stabilizer is completely removed. After the fabric dries, attach the flowers to the background with stitching or fusible web, and add stems and leaves if desired. Flower fabric by Bold Over Batiks.

Nancy Mambi is the creator of this delightful needle-felted flower piece. Hand-dyed wool has wool roving punched into it by hand; beading and hand embroidery add wonderful texture and interest. Notice how Nancy has mounted the wool background onto a red felt piece that peeks out along the edges and how she has backed the whole thing with another hand-dyed wool fabric to create a wall hanging with lots of body and wonderful eye appeal.

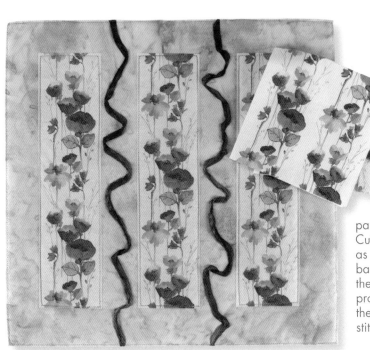

Get a pretty napkin at a luncheon? Turn it into wall hanging! Peel the top layer away from the rest of the napkin and press it flat with a steam iron (the perforations on the edges will be mostly hidden by the netting). Lay Mistyfuse adhesive web on the background fabric where the napkin parts will be. Don't worry if some of it is exposed because it won't show in the end. Place a sheet of baking parchment over the web and press. Peel the parchment off. Cut the napkin into separate flowers or stripes of flowers, as in the sample. Place the napkin parts on the fabric background, cover with parchment, and press to adhere them to the surface. Cover the fabric with sheer netting to protect the napkin, press again with parchment to adhere the netting to any exposed fusible web, and embellish with stitching and ribbons.

Leaves and Trees

Leaves and trees have been a popular subject for quilters throughout history. Antique quilts display pine trees made from tiny triangles, and blocks portray pieced maple leaves and palm tree fronds. Today, art quilters continue to convey the beauty and serenity of trees, using every technique imaginable—from photo realism to the barest abstract representations.

Mary Holland has used screen printed leaves to create these wall hangings, part of a larger grouping. Hand and machine stitching decorate the leaf blocks, which are placed on black fabric covered with exposed Mistyfuse web for visual texture. Batik fabrics finish out the background and borders while ribbons highlight embellishments of turquoise beads and beads made from Angelina film.

Tina Hughes again uses various simple printmaking techniques to create a complex surface and then reinforces the focal image with stitching and adds circular lines in the background. Ties added to the top enable a stick to be used as a hanger, which relates to the subject of the piece.

Tina Hughes uses real leaves laid on the copy machine to print onto photo transfer paper. The leaves are then cut apart and ironed onto different colored backgrounds. Her signature green colors with black-and-white accents create an interesting backdrop for the leaf blocks while simple stitching puts the emphasis on the leaves.

Freehand cut white silks to resemble snow drifts and cut tree trunks and branches out of black felt. Sprinkle Bo-Nash 007 bonding powder lightly over the background. Place the snow drifts and trees on top of the powder, and press the entire surface with a piece of baking parchment over the top. Satin-stitch or raw-edge appliqué the drifts and trees. Foil the exposed dots of adhesive powder to look like frost or stars.

Create a tree out of Lutradur by placing the interfacing on a piece of glass and cutting through it with a soldering iron or heat tool, giving it a slightly rough and natural-looking edge. Paint the tree with Dye-na-Flow paint and water and the let it dry. Fuse a large sheer leaf to the background and free-motion stitch outlines and veins into it and then topstitch the tree to the leaf. (Save the background Lutradur from cutting out the tree for another piece.) Fabric by Diane Bartels and Wendy Richardson.

Bleach pens are perfect for drawing trees onto black or dark fabric. Shake the pen before drawing. After the fabric shows signs of changing color, dunk it into warm soapy water to remove all the bleach. For archival-quality pieces, neutralize the bleach with Anti-Chlor dissolved in water. If you want a lighter colored tree instead of a reddish brown one, apply discharge paste with a dyer's syringe or needle-nose applicator and iron the fabric to activate the color removal process.

Lay a stencil on a pre-stretched canvas from an art supply store and tape it in place. With a palette knife or spatula, spread modeling paste in the openings, keeping the paste a uniform thickness. Remove the stencil and let the paste dry overnight. Spray the canvas with water and sponge-brush Dye-na-Flow paint over the surface, tipping the canvas to make the paint run and letting the colors mix. Be sure to paint the sides of the canvas, unless the piece will go into a frame. Stencil by www.cedarcanyontextiles.com.

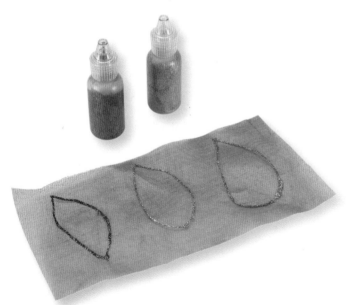

Use gorgeous metallic sheers to make an elegant little wall hanging. With glitter glue or other dimensional metallic paint, draw leaves onto metallic sheer fabric, let dry, and then cut out the leaves. The paint/glue will keep the edges from raveling.

Arrange the leaves on a "branch" made from fused fabric, couched yarn or ribbon, or twisted fabric and stitch down the centers to attach them to the background. Fabric by Diane Swallen.

Use leaves pressed in a phone book to make a nature print with discharge paste. Apply the paste to the back of the leaves with a sponge or sponge roller to create a nice texture. Place the coated leaves on black or dark fabric, cover with a paper towel to collect any wayward paste, and run over the paper towel with a brayer to print the leaf patterns. Work on an old towel or other slightly soft surface to facilitate a better print. Let the paste dry and then steam-iron to discharge the color from the fabric. Wash the fabric to remove any odor.

Create a background and then fuse a very simple pine tree on top. Trees, like flowers, are recognizable in their simplest form. Create a forest of trees, use a single tree with text, or stitch texture into the background.

Cut a tree stencil out of freezer paper or buy one from www.craftersworkshop.com. Iron the freezer paper stencil to fabric, or spray the plastic one with temporary adhesive like 404, let dry, and press onto the fabric. Spray over the stencil with spray fabric paint. Finish with a hand-drawn line of black ink or black stitching, if desired. Always use caution with sprays of any kind—they are best used outdoors.

Choose a medium- to light-colored background to represent forest and cut 8½" by 10½" (21.6 x 26.9cm) blocks. Draw or manipulate photos to give you black-and-white tree images and copy them onto photo transfer paper. Iron the tree images to some of the blocks. On other blocks, cut vertical and diagonal lines through the block and piece in 1" (2.5 cm)-wide tree trunks, pressing the seam allowances toward the tree (the block should remain the same size.) Arrange the blocks on the design wall and stitch together. Fabric by Diane Swallen and Dianne McAnaney; images by Doroth Mayer.

Paint a tree onto a green background using Dye-na-Flow. Let dry. Screen print, stamp, stencil, or paint freehand leaves with opaque fabric paint. Heat set.

An oddly colored bundle of hand-dyed fabric purchased at a show inspired this tree quilt. A sampler quilt top made entirely of half-square triangles and plain alternate blocks was completed first and then cotton organza was dyed to complement the colors. The tree was cut out and appliquéd over the quilt top, after which the quilting was done following the piecing lines of the blocks, disregarding the tree completely. The quilt reminded me of the painted desert of Colorado, so is called Ghost Tree.

Draw leaf outlines with stencils onto the release paper of Wonder-Under fusible web. Fuse the web to black fabric and cut out the leaves on the lines. Remove the release paper and fuse the leaves to a colorful background fabric, using linear or radial symmetry as your guide. Quilt over the whole surface in a grid of casual straight lines, which will secure the leaves and add a secondary design. Stencils by www.cedarcanyontextiles.com.

Instead of black leaves cut with stencils, cut freehand leaves from beautiful fabrics that have been backed with Wonder-Under. Fuse the leaves to rectangles of fabric that have also been backed with fusible web. Fuse the blocks to a black background and quilt with a grid.

Split Blocks

Making an appliquéd quilt block and then cutting into two or four sections is a fun way to create seren-dipitous new blocks. You can fuse or raw-edge appliqué and the point is not to cut perfect shapes!

How to Make a Split Block Quilt Top

1 With baking parchment placed on top, fuse Mistyfuse web to the back of several fabrics. Freehand cut a circle and fuse it to a square or rectangular background block. Cut outlines from a contrasting fabric and fuse them to the outside edge of the circle. Repeat for three more blocks.

2 Cut through the center of the blocks, and mix and match the halves to make new ones. Piece the selected halves to a 1" (2.5 cm)-wide strip of contrasting fabric and press the seam allowances toward the strip. Arrange the blocks and sew them together with lattice strips and borders. Fabrics by Dianne McAnaney, Diane Bartels, Lunn Fabrics, Wendy Richardson.

Another Version

1 Cut three sizes of circles without fusible on the back of the fabric. Choosing fabrics that ravel (cotton muslin or silk Dupioni) adds texture and interest. Pile a large, medium, and small circle on top of each other and topstitch the edge of the small circle to a background square. Repeat for as many blocks as you want in your quilt. Note: These are 6½" (16.5 cm) blocks to start. If you make your blocks larger, sew around all the circle edges.

2 Cut through each block in both directions. Combine parts of different squares to make new blocks and sew them together. Press the seams open to reduce bulk. Sew the blocks in rows and assemble the quilt top. Brush the edges of the circles to fray them for a softer look. Fabric by Marit Lee Kucera, www.m-artistic.com.

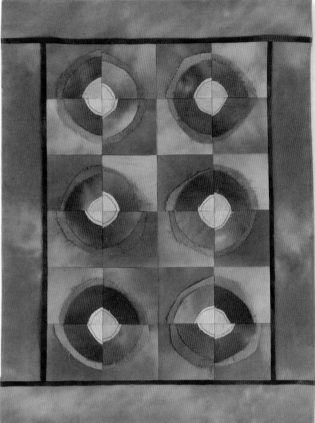

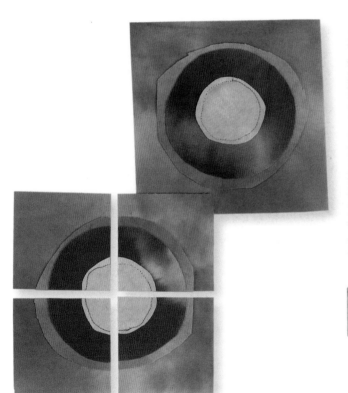

FIVE PROJECTS

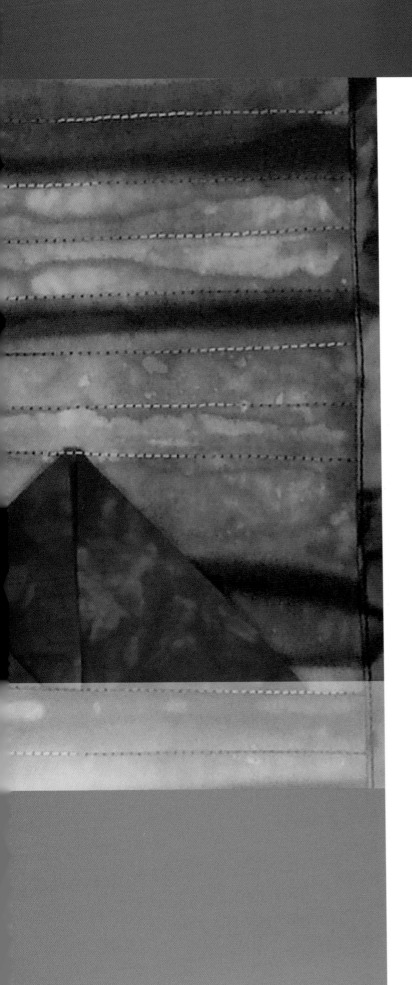

If you have never made an art quilt before or have always followed a pattern, the next section is for you. Even though materials are listed and steps are spelled out, feel free to change these specifications as you please—you are the artist! What's important is that the quilt shows quality construction, will hold up to the use for which it is intended, and that the composition and design are good. Use the best materials you can find, or get out the dyes or paints and make your own one-of-a-kind fabrics. Look at the samples throughout the book to see how exquisite fabrics can turn a simple design into a piece of art.

There are several processes that go into making a quilt—design; material choices; piecing, appliqué, or surface design; layering; stitching/quilting; embellishing; finishing the edges; and making the quilt ready for hanging. All of them are important to a successful project. Fortunately, as art quilters, we hold to few rules and have multiple techniques to choose from for each process. We can emphasize our strong points and simplify the parts we don't enjoy as much. Most of all, savor the journey. Think of these projects as starting points for your own creative ideas—after all, the term art quilt implies that the piece is one of a kind, so make it your own!

Waves of Texture

30" (76 cm) square before quilting

YOU WILL NEED

- ¾ yd (0.7 m) of fabric for center
- ¾ yd (0.7 m) of fabric for borders and binding
- ½ yd (0.46) each of two fabrics for waves
- 1 yd (0.9 m) of fabric for back
- crib-sized (45" x 60" [114.5 x 152.5 cm]) Hobbs cotton/poly fusible batting
- thin yarns, perle cottons, and cords
- threads—sewing, quilting, and invisible
- cheesecloth or silk organza dyed, painted, or left white like foam if doing an ocean wave
- pins
- rotary cutter and mat
- 24" (61 cm) acrylic ruler
- white chalk pencil
- sewing machine with zigzag function

Cutting

1 Cut a 24½" (62.2 cm) square of the center fabric. Cut crosswise strips of border fabric, four 3½" (8.9 cm) wide and four 2" (5.1 cm) wide.

Sewing

2 Cut two border strips to 24½" (62.2 cm) long and sew to the top and bottom of the center square.

3 Cut two border strips to 30½" (77.5 cm) long and sew to the sides of the center square. Press.

4 Lay the quilt top over the fusible batting and steam iron. Pull the batting off the ironing board cover and place the quilt sandwich on the design wall.

Making waves

5 Fold one of the wave fabrics in half the long way, right sides together. Draw a wavy line the long way on the fabric and another line 4" to 5" (10 to 12.5 cm) away. Place a strip of batting underneath the fabric, steam, pin, and stitch on the two lines through all the layers. Cut away the excess batting and fabric, leaving ¼" (6 mm) seam allowances outside the stitching lines. Repeat for the other wave fabric.

6 Turn the waves right sides out through the ends and press flat. Couch yarns and cords along the length of the waves using invisible thread and a medium-width zigzag stitch (as shown in these smaller samples). If you have a couching foot for your machine, feed the thinner cords through the hole in the foot.

7 Lay the waves diagonally across the quilt top until you are pleased with the arrangement. Pin and remove the quilt top from the design wall. Couch a cord along the sides of the waves, gathering strips of cheesecloth or organza underneath the edges as you sew.

8 Steam the backing to the batting and quilt the areas around the waves, catching the cheesecloth. Straighten the edges of the quilt and bind, enclosing the ends of the waves at the same time. Leave the ends of the cheesecloth or organza free, or include in the binding. Sign your name and the date on the *front* of the quilt—it is a piece of art!

5

6

7

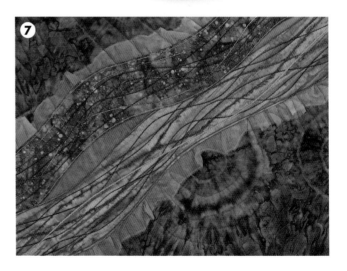

Lining Up

11" x 40" (28 x 101.5 cm) before quilting

Cutting

1 Cut an 11" x 40" (28 x 101.5 cm) piece of striped fabric (fabric by Diane Swallen).

2 Cut the fabric piece into five 8" (20.3 cm) sections.

3 Cut one or two accent fabrics into a total of six 5" (12.7 cm) squares.

4 Cut one or two accent fabrics into two 4½"x 9" (11.4 x 23 cm) rectangles.

Sewing

5 Make six prairie points by folding the 5" (12.7 cm) squares of accent fabric in half horizontally. Fold the two sides down so the folded edges meet in the center, making a triangle. Press.

6 Fold the accent rectangles in half, right sides together. Sew across the ends with a ¼" (6 mm) seam and turn right sides out. Press.

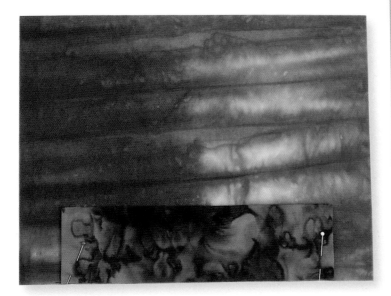

YOU WILL NEED

- ⅝ yd (0.34 m) of striped fabric
- ½ yd (0.46 m) of backing and binding fabric
- small pieces of coordinating fabrics for accents
- sewing and quilting thread
- 12" x 41" (30.5 x 104 cm) piece of Hobbs cotton/poly fusible batting
- pins
- rotary cutter and mat
- 24" (61 cm) acrylic ruler
- sewing machine

7 Place the five striped fabric sections on the design wall and arrange the accent pieces between them. Line up the raw edges of the accents with the raw edges of the striped sections, pin, and stitch together. Press the seams toward the bottom.

8 Lay the quilt top on the batting and steam. Quilt the layers, catching the points and corners of the accent pieces. The sample is quilted with the walking foot and casual straight lines (no marking needed). The lines are worked back and forth to avoid pushing the top fabric out of alignment, which might happen if all the lines were quilted in one direction.

9 Trim the batting and straighten the edges. Iron the backing to the back.

10 Trim the backing fabric to ⅝" (1.6 cm) away from the edges of the quilt top. Iron under ¼" (6 mm), fold over onto the quilt top, and topstitch the edge.

This piece lends itself to embellishments: use beading to tack down the prairie points, position beads to emerge out of the pockets made by the accent rectangles, or embroider on the accent rectangles. Poetry could be printed onto the main fabric or stamps could be used to add images.

Lines and Leaves

30" x 42" (76.2 x 106.7 cm) before quilting

Cutting

1 Press the background fabric and cut to 30" x 42" (76.2 x 106.7 cm).
Cut four 2" (5.1 cm)-wide strips of binding crosswise on the binding fabric.
Blocks will be cut as you go.

YOU WILL NEED

- small pieces of cotton fabric for blocks and leaves, including some black for lines
- Wonder-Under fusible web
- ⅞ yd (0.8 m) of black fabric for background
- ⅞ yd (0.8 m) of fabric for backing
- ⅓ yd (0.3 m) of fabric for binding
- crib-sized (45" x 60" [114.5 x 152.5 cm]) Hobbs cotton/poly fusible batting
- thread for quilting
- rotary cutter and mat
- acrylic ruler
- scissors

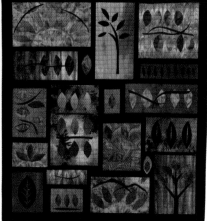

Lines and Leaves III is another version of this quilt that highlights hand-dyed and commercial fabrics.

Assembly

2 Press the background fabric and place it on the design wall. Prepare the block, black line, and leaf fabrics by ironing Wonder-Under to the backs. Use a dry iron and be sure to iron the edges thoroughly.

3 Choose a pleasing combination of fabrics with contrast in value, color, or texture. Cut one fabric into a rectangular block. Cut the other into simple leaf shapes (refer to the sample for ideas) that will fit onto the block, and peel off the release paper from the back. Iron the leaves to the block.

4 Cut black lines and iron them over the leaves. Repeat for more blocks. Note: The leaves are very irregular in shape and size which add interest. Use your imagination to create unique combinations of leaves and lines, adding branches and trees if you like.

5 Peel the release paper from the backs of the blocks and arrange them on the background fabric, placing a pin at the top. Fill in the background with blocks, leaving a 2½" (6.4 cm) strip of background all around the edges for a visual border. Note: You may want to mark a light chalk line around the edge at the 2½" (6.4 cm) measurement. Carefully remove the background from the wall and place on a flat surface. Pin the blocks to the background, making sure the spaces between the blocks are even and the border areas are straight. Iron the blocks to the background using steam, removing the pins as you go.

6 Fuse the quilt top and back to the batting using steam. With a walking foot, quilt a grid of casual straight lines over the quilt surface. Start the grid by marking center lines horizontally and vertically with a chalk pencil. After quilting those lines, simply quilt somewhat parallel lines in both directions, changing sections often so the quilt stays square.

7 Trim the edges of the quilt and bind with 2" (5 cm)-wide strips. If any leaf or line tips have loosened, glue them down with tiny dots of white glue or fabric glue.

Layers of Letters

Variable size, sample is approximately 15" x 17½" (38 x 44.5 cm)

YOU WILL NEED

- background fabric larger than your stencil
- border and backing/binding fabric
- batting
- large paper cutout from a scrapbook store or large plastic letter stencil (or paper one from the office supply store)
- tape
- Lumiere paint by Jacquard or other opaque paint
- blank silk screen
- squeegee or credit card
- ExtravOrganza inkjet fabric sheets
- Mistyfuse adhesive web
- baking parchment
- sponge brush
- stencils
- permanent marker
- sheer fabrics in coordinating colors

Surface Design

1 Place the stencil on the background fabric and tape in place. If the screen mesh is larger than the stencil, tape off the areas extending beyond the design by sticking masking tape to the back of the screen (the side that will lie against the fabric). Place the screen over the stencil, pour paint on one end of the screen, and squeegee paint over the stencil design. Do not worry if the print is not perfect because you will be layering over it. Pull the screen and stencil off of the fabric and wash immediately. Let dry and then iron the paint to set.

2 Type words or letters into the computer (play with different fonts) and print out on an ExtravOrganza fabric sheet. Let dry and then peel off the backing paper, keeping the grain of the fabric as straight as possible. Lightly fuse the printed sheet to Mistyfuse adhesive web, sandwiched by baking parchment to protect the ironing board and iron. Cut out the words or letters.

3 Add letters or words to sheer fabrics using Lumiere paint, a sponge brush, and stencils. Or use a permanent marker with a smaller stencil. Back with Mistyfuse as before (or not, if the sheer has enough body by itself) and cut out.

Sewing

4 Arrange the cutout letters over the background fabric and then fuse or pin in place.

5 Stitch borders onto the background and layer with batting and backing.

6 Quilt around the letters and bind.

Fence and Lattice

Variable size, sample is 35" (89 cm) square

Since demonstrating gelatin printing generates lots of 9" x 11" (23 x 28 cm) samples that are related in color and design (these are made with orange plastic construction fencing), I looked for a way to use some in a wall hanging. The first step was placing all the samples on the design wall and determining how many were usable and what configuration would work—three blocks by three, four blocks by three, etc.

Cutting and Sewing

1 Draw a rough sketch to determine how much lattice fabric will be needed to separate the blocks and how much border fabric will be needed. The blocks in the sample were printed on an 8" (20.5 cm) square gelatin pad, so they needed to be cut down to 8½" (21.5 cm) square, which made the finished block size 8" (20.5 cm). That size of block needs only a 1½" or 2" (3.8 or 5.1 cm) lattice strip to separate it from the next block—otherwise the lattice is out of proportion. The border can be half as wide as the block size or narrower. Corner squares added to the lattice and border allow you to use one or two more fabrics if you like, or they can be eliminated.

YOU WILL NEED

- blocks left over from surface design or other experiments
- lattice and border fabrics
- thread for sewing and quilting
- batting and backing fabric slightly larger than the quilt top
- binding fabric

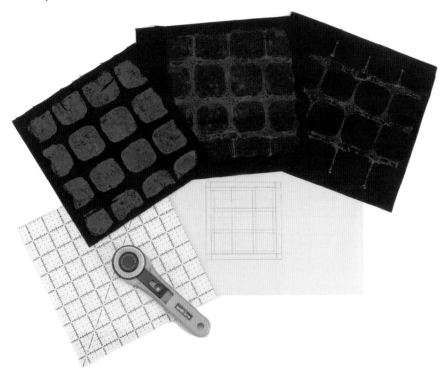

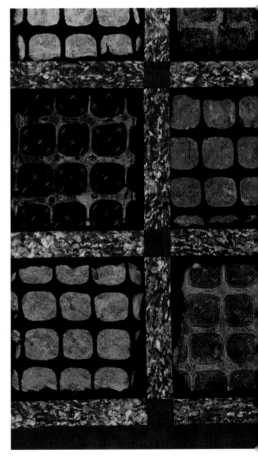

2 Cut the lattice and borders according to your calculations. Remember to add ¼" (6 mm) seam allowances to your measurements. Cut the blocks down to size. Put everything back on the design wall and take down the parts in sections to sew them together. Press the seam allowances away from the blocks.

3 Layer the quilt with batting and backing, and quilt by hand and/or machine. The sample is quilted in the seam lines by machine. The blocks are quilted by hand with long stitches.

FINISHING THE ART QUILT

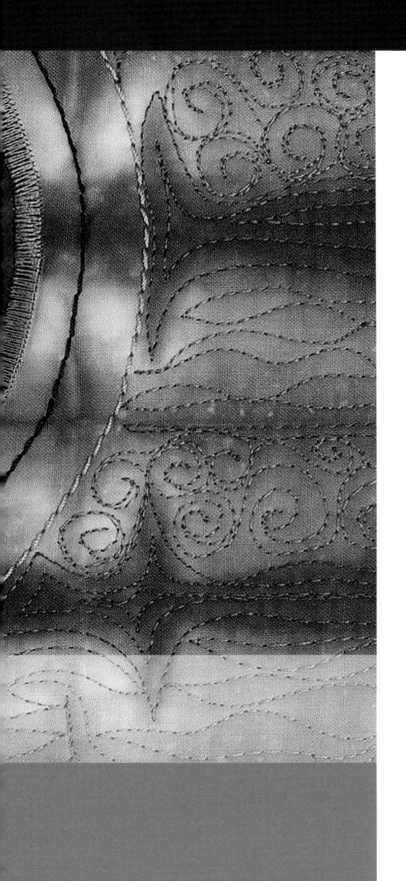

Without quality stitching, embellishment, and edge finishing, the most elegant and artistic quilt top will not show to its best advantage. Texture, detail, dimension, and so on are all developed with the finishing techniques chosen. For some people, the quilting is their favorite part of the whole art quilting process, and hand-stitching is enjoying a big revival. For others, altering the finished piece with paint or discharge paste is both a frightening and exciting process. Binding is even being diversified and breaking all the old rules.

Substrates

The term substrate has recently appeared in the literature relating to collage and other mixed-media artwork, whereas it mainly referred to biology in the past. It refers to the background or foundation material used for making a piece of art, whether it is stitched or not.

We will talk about substrates in reference to art quilting and how it can change a quilt from a soft flexible textile made with thin cotton fabric and thread, as in a traditional quilt, to a rigid piece requiring special techniques to stitch through. Be aware of the considerations necessary to ship pieces that are stiff and must be kept flat—you may have to create a special container and ensure that the people who are hanging a show know that the piece must always be flat.

Cindy Trainor's piece from the Fiber Edge exhibit (pages 168 to 177) shows an extreme and wonderful example of an art quilt for the twenty-first century! Screen, hardware, metal sheeting, and a box frame demonstrate how beautifully metal can be screwed and bracketed together to execute the elements and textures of a quilt without using a single piece of fabric or thread.

Most quilters will stay closer to home when trying out new substrates other than the usual batting and backing fabric. If doing thread painting, Timtex or Peltex (heavy interfacing used in hat brims and fabric bowls) make an ideal substrate because the fabric won't pucker when the extensive stitching is done. A layer of fusible web between the fabric and the interfacing ensures that the fabric will stay in place and no hoop will be needed to stabilize the fabric. The finished piece will be very stiff and, although the dimension of quilting over batting is not possible, there is no problem machine stitching through the thicker layers. Hand-stitching would require lots of patience but would be possible—for difficult areas, use a needle-nose pliers to pull the needle through, especially if using heavy thread. If a substrate is extremely heavy, use an awl or stiletto to make holes first and then stitch through them.

Synthetic felt, the kind made of recycled plastic bottles, makes a quick and effective substrate and is easy to sew through or glue onto. The felt is sold in 9" x 12" (22.9 x 30.5 cm) pieces or ones twice that size.

(continued)

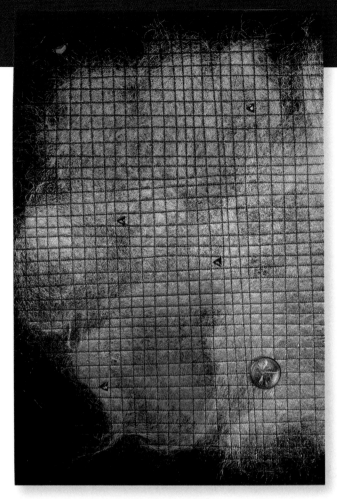

Here, Angelina was made into a large sheet, placed on the felt, covered with tulle, and stitched in a grid. A glass dragonfly button and some small prism glass beads were sewn or glued onto the surface. The piece could be matted and framed or bound and hung as is. Hand-stitching could be done through the felt, but a stab stitch would be required because the substrate cannot be gathered onto the needle for a normal running stitch.

This cardinal picture (Sarah Archbold) was printed onto photo transfer fabric and then fused to a piece of heavy Peltex to allow for heavy stitching. Some artists choose to completely cover the original photo with stitching.

Sheer substrates are completely different from stiff ones and may require stretching while working on them. That can be accomplished with an embroidery hoop or a pin board (a piece of foam core or cardboard that the fabric can be pinned to).

Papers, handmade and imported, are becoming popular elements in art quilts, because wall hangings do not get washed and the paper acts just like fabric during construction but adds fantastic texture. Edges can be torn and left unfinished and paper can be either glued or sewn. Use longer stitch lengths to avoid cutting through the paper and make sure the paper can support the weight of whatever you attach to it. The paper can be backed with stiff fusible interfacing to make it sturdier or glued to mat board for support as soon as the stitching is completed. Of course, using layers of paper and sheer fabrics with fluid acrylic medium to make cloth/paper lamination makes an extremely strong substrate but expect a very stiff result.

Here the sheer was stiff enough to work on as is, but the other sheer elements were fused down before stitching to avoid slippage. To allow light to show through, no backing was added.

Fabric by Wendy Richardson and Rosemary Kessler.

Machine Quilting

Once you have your art quilt top completed, it is time to make lots of decisions about how to finish it. For example, will you use batting, backing, embellishment or not, hand or machine stitching, beading, painting, discharge, thread painting, or many other options? Decisions about final display options can wait until the edge finishes are considered.

Let's start with machine quilting. There are numerous books about how to do it and what patterns to use. It's best to take a class from an experienced instructor because seeing is so much better than reading. Nothing will replace lots of practice, however.

Styles change every few years and it's curious that the current trends are hand-stitching with huge stitches and machine quilting in intricate patterns with miniscule spaces between the lines of stitch. The intense machine quilting is definitely a major secondary design element as opposed to a functional fastening of the layers together, which formerly was a matter of adding warmth to a decorative bedcover.

There are differing opinions on whether extreme quilting is attractive or not, but it is always eye catching when seen in a show. My concern is that quilters with less experience will feel intimidated to quilt their own tops, and while there are numerous talented machine quilters who work for hire, part of the satisfaction of making a quilt is the stitching of the layers. Don't feel that intricate free-motion quilting is the only route to making a successful wall hanging—in fact, very few pieces in this book are extensively stitched. Time factors and interest in different facets of making a quilt may determine how it is finished. For many quilters, the designing and selecting/making of the materials are the most exciting parts of constructing an art quilt and the quilting is a relaxing time when the decisions are made and they can watch the textures of the stitching emerge without the stress of creating another whole design dimension.

Some of the smaller projects shown previously have been quilted as they were assembled. Following this approach, if there are fused patterns that need topstitching on the edges, you could do it through the batting and avoid having to quilt around the motif later. Or if a ribbon needs to be fastened down, stitch through the batting at the same time to give the ribbon more dimension—stitching down the middle raises up the sides, and stitching down the sides puffs up the center. Often the backing is left off when the stitching/quilting is done in this way, so the binding can be part of the backing process. Only a small wall hanging should be handled like this, because the weight of a larger quilt needs the support of a stitched backing. This method also allows for a cleaner looking back should the assembly require knots or traveling with the needle to various areas. Using a high-quality fusible batting, like Hobbs 80 percent cotton/20 percent polyester batting, makes adding the batting to the back of the quilt top very quick and easy. After the layers are quilted, the backing fabric can be ironed to the back of the quilt for the binding process.

Basics that can never be stressed enough:

- Keep the quilting consistently dense for a flat quilt, especially important for wall hangings. If the interior area of the quilt is heavily quilted, the borders must be also.

- A steam iron can be used after the quilting is done to flatten out minor unevenness. Be sure to use a large ironing surface (even the floor) and leave the quilt in place until it is completely dry.

- Use only thin batting for a wall hanging—you are going for texture and dimension, not warmth.

- Make sure your sewing machine, chair, and lighting are all comfortably arranged and at the right height.

- Polish the sewing machine table with furniture wax so the quilt moves around easily.

- Remove all cats from the quilt.

- Take frequent breaks to loosen tight muscles and wear quilting gloves to help maneuver the quilt.

- After the stitching is completed and the quilt is steamed flat, it can be placed on a gridded cutting mat and straightened with the rotary cutter before binding. There shouldn't be more than a ¼" (6 mm) deviation from square, but on a smaller wall hanging, even that can be noticeable.

Here, on "Timeless," the grid quilting was done before the napkin, doily, and other elements were added with stitching and fusing. The stitched grid adds interest, texture, and function as it makes a sturdy substrate for the other elements.

For the most relaxing approach to machine quilting the three layers together, use a walking foot, which keeps the guidance of the machine's feed dogs in place. Stitching can be done in the seam lines of the patchwork if there are some present, but many art quilts are appliqué or surface design and there are no seams involved. No changes to the settings of the machine are needed—straight stitches of ten per inch (2.5 cm) are pretty standard and threads can vary (cotton, rayon, polyester, silk), usually with a cotton thread on the bobbin. A change in needle may be necessary for thicker or finicky threads. After basting the layers of the quilt together with fusible batting and a steam iron, safety pins, or thread basting, stitch a line down the center of the quilt horizontally and vertically to stabilize it. Stitch parallel to the two starting lines at intervals of your choosing—closer together for small pieces and further apart for large quilts. The lines do not have to be perfectly straight and, in fact, will be more interesting if they wander a bit. Change directions often to keep the quilt in square.

(continued)

A quilt by Sue Kelly illustrates how a piece of discharged fabric can become artful through the use of simple quilting, both in matching and metallic thread. The lines of quilting follow the lines made by zigzag-stitching black fabric between layers of plastic and then brushing bleach or discharge paste over the lines so it just goes through the holes in the plastic to remove the color.

This piece reminds us that there can be lines in just one direction. Diagonal lines are often very effective as a simple secondary element if they are superimposed over horizontal and vertical patterns, especially if executed with heavy thread in a contrasting color.

Gentle curves can be accomplished with a walking foot, whereas sharp curves need to be done with a darning foot and dropped feed dogs. Test your project to determine which method is easier. Marking the curves on tracing paper and pinning the paper to the quilt will ensure that a slight deviation in the stitch line won't be revealed by an exposed pencil mark and will result in a consistent pattern if doing cables or circles.

A wall hanging can be quilted in one huge spiral, which unifies a design and is fun to do, even though it is somewhat time consuming. Start with a chalk circle about 6" (15.2 cm) in diameter (the smallest circle you can comfortably do with a walking foot) and quilt along the line only for a short distance—the stitching will need to be about ⅝" to ¾" (1.6 to 1.9 cm) away from the chalk line by the time you get back to the starting point.

Keep going around the spiral until you reach the sides of the quilt top and then fill in the corners. The trick to keeping the circle as round as possible is to look ahead of where you are stitching to avoid repeating a deviation in the previous round. To complete the inside of the circle, use a darning foot and dropped feed dogs to free-motion stitch the rest of the spiral. Remember that using the walking foot requires feeding the quilt straight through under the presser foot, so this method only works on a small piece that can be turned freely.

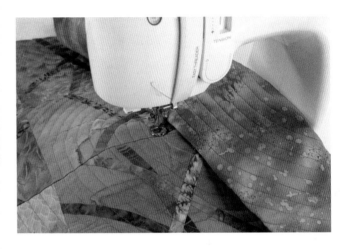

Another easy and relaxing way to use the walking foot to do an overall quilting pattern is to hang the quilt top on the wall and draw a curvy line with a chalk pencil. Quilt along the line and then stitch the remaining lines by staying approximately parallel to the first but fanning out the ends of the lines for flair.

(continued)

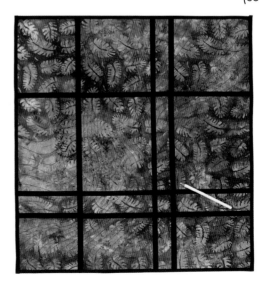

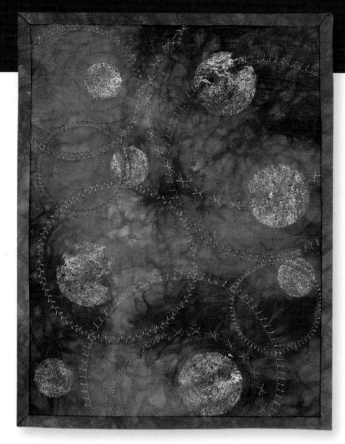

Switching to free-motion quilting, where the machine does not guide the movement of the quilt, requires practice and lots of doodle cloths or quilts for the dog bed. Drop the feed dogs and you have total freedom to go any direction and be as creative as you like. The quilt no longer has to be turned to follow a circular pattern but can be oriented one way while you sew sideways, forward, and backward to follow the design. Don't worry if your stitches are not regular in length to begin with—work on developing your own rhythm and comfort zone.

Sue Kelly's circle quilt displays foiled circles, circles of machine embroidery, and very subtle circles of machine quilting in invisible thread, which give the piece texture without adding another noticeable design element.

Try quilting something from the back, following a print fabric as your pattern. Sew around the edges of the top so you know the exact area to quilt and start stitching in the center to stabilize the layers. Wear quilting gloves to help move the quilt when doing free-motion quilting, and take frequent breaks.

This fun piece by Sue Kelly was quilted with a wave pattern and a few spirals around the three ginko leaves. After the quilting was complete, Sue filled in the leaves with Paintstik for a simple yet dramatic design.

Sue Kelly's little discharge quilt benefits from lots of quilting, but rather than standing out so much that it distracts the viewer, it adds interest and texture. The patterns chosen emphasize the discharged designs and yet unify the different elements.

Hand-dyed fabric was featured by Sue as she added a large circle, which she outlined with straight and satin stitching and then quilted very heavily, highlighting features in the fabric and filling in other areas with rock, swirl, and wave quilting. This type of quilt will please the quilter who loves free-motion quilting, as the quilt top is quickly made and then the fun begins.

Another discharge (the black fabric was poked through the sides of a laundry basket and sprayed with bleach water) piece by Sue shows black-on-black stitching around the white motifs except for the two parts she decided to highlight with red metallic thread—one of the abstract patterns and one mark that looks vaguely like a figure. Red metallic fabric used for a tiny piping along the binding adds to the wonderful impact found in this tiny quilt.

Adding Shading and Details

Besides stitching to hold the layers together, to add secondary designs, and to add texture, stitching can be used on the art quilt to add shading and detail to appliquéd or printed images. Sometimes these steps are done on only the top, but they can also be done after the layers are assembled, making a sturdier base on which to work.

Karen Wallach likes to use her drawings to create quilting designs before she starts to stitch on the actual piece. Here her apples from the sketchbook chapter (page 42) appear again with differently colored marker used to indicate different colors of thread. Crosshatching (stitching in both directions) is based on an imaginary light source coming from one direction, so it replicates shadows on the three-dimensional objects.

Karen practices on a doodle cloth so she can make sure her fruit turns out to be apples and not tomatoes! Using woolly nylon thread along with regular cotton thread makes a darker line than sewing only with the cotton.

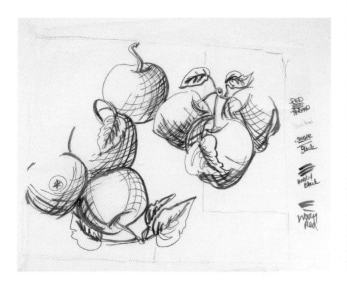

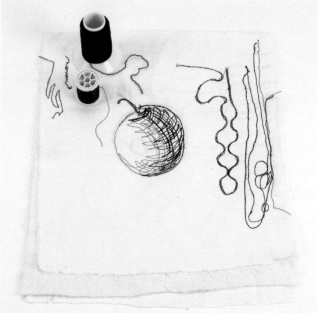

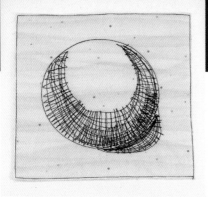
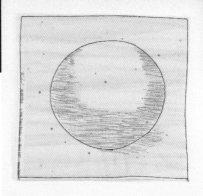

Practice adding shading to a simple shape by making five samples for your reference file. Draw a 6" (15.2 cm) circle on five 9" (22.9 cm) squares of light-colored fabric, steam-iron to fusible batting, and add a backing to the other side of the batting. Quilt around the edges to stabilize them and outline the circle. For the first sample, stitch crosshatching around the lower side of the circle, imagining a light source at the top left of the square. Drop the feed dogs and hand-guide the machine. You don't have to break the stitching as you go back and forth in one direction but consider it a large zigzag. Then do the second direction the same manner.

Thread painting is a more about adding texture than shading and goes only one direction, again done with the feed dogs dropped. Add stitching to the ball in the same way as before but cover most of the fabric underneath with thread. Keep the motor of the machine going at a rapid speed to maintain a short stitch length while moving the quilt back and forth under the needle. Thread painting is usually done in almost matching thread for a more realistic look than crosshatching, which is done with contrasting thread.

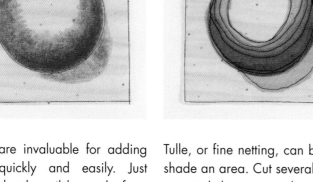
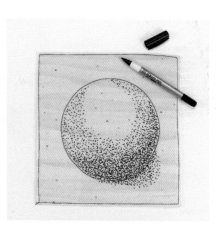

Paintstiks are invaluable for adding shading quickly and easily. Just remember that the quilt has to dry for a couple of days before handling. Peel the dry skin off the tip of the paintstik and then gently rub paint onto the ball to create shadow. After the paint dries, iron it to make it permanent.

Tulle, or fine netting, can be used to shade an area. Cut several circles of net, stitch the interior edge of the light area on the first layer of net, and then cut out the light area. Add a second layer of net, stitch the interior edge, and cut out the excess. The third and fourth layers will be smaller and smaller as your build up darker and darker values for dimension. After the last layer is on, stitch around the outer edges of the net pieces along the outline of the circle.

Dots made with a permanent marker are a fun way to shade an area. Change the spaces between the dots to alter the darkness of the shadows.
(continued)

For adding details, quilting can act as an accent or can actually be the vehicle for attaching appliqué elements to the quilt. Cut a leaf pattern from freezer paper and iron the background paper onto the fabric to Paintstik a shadow on the background fabric. Cut a leaf with the actual pattern and fuse it over the shadow leaf. Add veins and outlines by dropping the feed dogs and doing free-motion quilting. Consider the machine a pencil and draw lines, not worrying about perfection but adding an organic kind of stitch. Do not draw a line to follow because it will be very hard to stay on and takes away the fun of winging it.

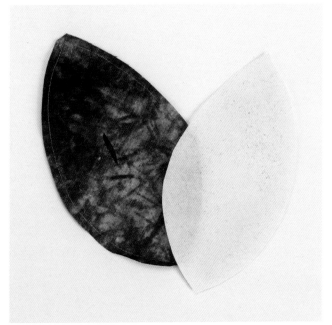

Cut two leaves with seam allowances, place right sides together, and stitch around on the seam line. Cut a hole in one of the layers and turn the leaf right side out through the hole. Press. Sew the leaf to the quilt by just stitching the veins, leaving the edges of the leaf free. This would also be a good way to add the hair to a face appliqué or the wings on a bird.

Use the leaf pattern (made from cardboard or manila folder) to starch under the seam allowances of the fabric. Use an invisible thread and blind-hem stitch to attach the leaf to the background fabric. Add detail with contrasting thread.

Hand-Stitching

Those who enjoy handwork will be pleased to discover a whole new emphasis on hand-quilting with large stitches and prominent thread. Since many quilt tops are about surface design and less about appliqué or piecing, big hand-stitches lend wonderful texture to whole cloth or nearly whole cloth pieces.

Embroidery stitches of all kinds can be used, but most often straight stitch, running stitch, cross stitch, French knots, and seed stitch are used and rules are ignored. Threads can be perle cotton, size 12 variegated cotton threads, or any sewing thread. No special needle is required since you're not going for tiny stitches, but embroidery or crewel needles with large eyes allow easy threading for larger threads. Backing fabric should be not too tightly woven, so stick to sheeting and broadcloth instead of pima cotton. Batting should be thin and not too dense. Since it will be difficult to bury larger knots in the batting as in fine hand-quilting, you may want to make them a design feature hidden among French knots or leave them exposed on the back where they will be hidden when the art quilt is hung.

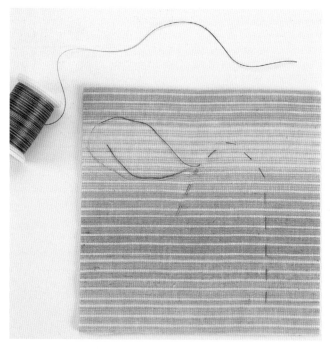

Straight stitch is plain stitches with spaces equal to stitch length, lined up or not.

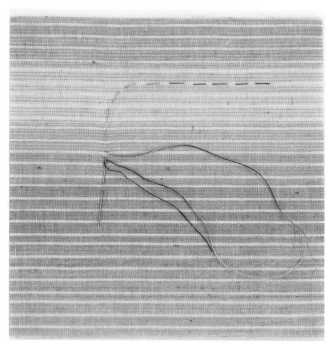

Running stitch is a line of stitches with smaller spaces in between.

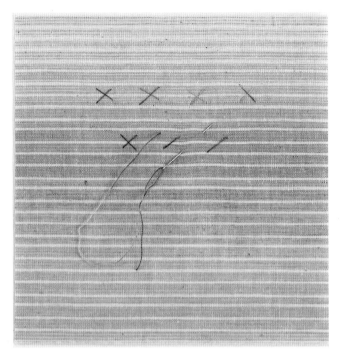

Cross stitch is little Xs, scattered or in lines.

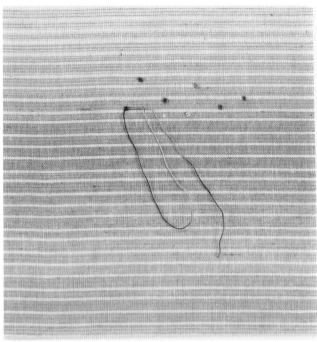

French knots wind the thread around the needle to make little 3D dots. Come up from the back, wind the thread three to five times around the needle, and go back down through the fabric close to the place you came out, holding the winds so they stay tight to the needle.

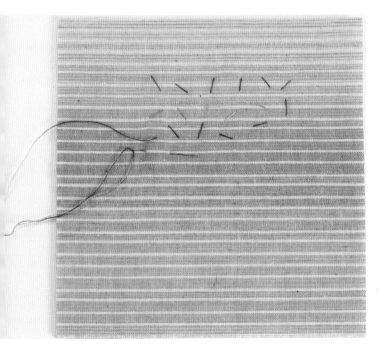

Seed stitch is short straight stitches going in every direction and used as fill.

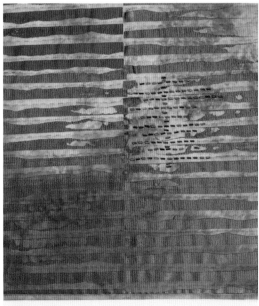

This screen printed top with beads already applied is best hand-quilted with straight stitches, avoiding the stiffer painted lines and beaded area, which are raised up by the stitching around them.

Embellishing the Finished Quilt

Once the layers are stitched together, the art quilt can still be embellished! Doing surface design over the quilt or beading on it adds an unexpected surprise and wonderful visual and actual texture. It is best to make a small swatch with your materials and stitching so you can test the results before touching the finished quilt.

The finished quilt can be altered by changing the color with discharge paste. Test a corner or scrap to make sure the new color will be pleasing next to the original one. Then gather your courage and sponge roll over the quilt, either parts or the whole top.

Sue Kelly's discharged quilt sampler shows what was originally just a piece of black fabric. The patterns were quilted on the black with reddish-brown thread and then all the blocks except the upper left one were discharged with paste that had Jacquard Textile Color paint added to it so the color was removed and replaced in one operation. The upper right block was painted with Lumiere metallic paint by Jacquard.

Here a ruler was held on the quilt while the roller was run in stripes next to it so the original and altered colors would contrast. By using a roller, the high points of the quilt are discharged while the valleys of the quilting lines remain unchanged. After the paste dries, iron the quilt with steam to remove the color. Quilting by Sue Kelly.

Many of the samples shown in this book are small and allow for lots of play and experimentation. Join with a group of friends and propose challenges to each other that encourage creativity and often end up being the focus of a guild program or small exhibit.

Fabric by Linda Davis, quilting by Sue Kelly.

Going over the finished quilt with Paintstik can make a spectacular difference. You can isolate certain areas and carefully fill in those places with the tip of the Paintstik, or peel off the skin from the side of a Paintstik and rub over the entire surface, which highlights the raised places and leaves the valleys of the stitch lines the original color. The Paintstik tends to be heavier along the stitching, emphasizing the shapes even more. Remember that the Paintstik needs to dry for two or three days before handling.

For a very different look, choose a high-contrast fabric paint like Lumiere and sponge roll over the quilt. Roll the sponge roller on a piece of glass or plastic after loading with paint to push the paint evenly into the sponge; this will help avoid blobs of excess paint at the beginning of your strokes across the quilt. Push only hard enough to unload the paint but not to fill the valleys made by the stitching. This sample illustrates various amounts of pressure used.

Beading is a beautiful addition to a finished art quilt. Wendie Zekowski has added seed beads to a fourth piece of Sue Kelly quilted fabric and elevated it to an elegant work of art. Not only texture is added, but also light reflections.

Sue has added handmade fabric beads to this stamped and quilted piece. The beads are made from cotton strips rolled around bamboo skewers and then wrapped with trims and foiled. Glass bugle beads and large round beads are also added to the fascinating mix.

Binding and Other Edge Finishes

You probably have a favorite edge finish for your quilts, but you may be looking for something faster or that doesn't require hand-stitching, especially for small quilts that are addictive to make and don't warrant a traditional hand-stitched binding. Just keep in mind that the binding or edge finish can make or break a piece of art and is just as important to execute well as all the other elements in a quilt.

Many of the samples in previous sections have been quilted without a backing to allow the binding to be included with the backing fabric. The quilt top is basted to the batting by steaming to fusible batting, pinning, or thread basting. For this method, follow these steps.

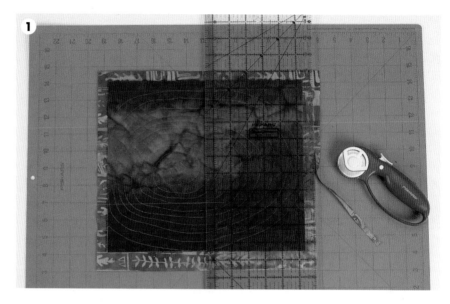

1 After the quilting is finished, trim the quilt/batting sandwich by laying it on a large cutting mat and rotary cutting it so the sides are square. Steam or baste the backing onto the reverse side of the batting (backing should be about an inch [2.5 cm] larger on all sides). Trim the backing to an exact ⅝" (1.6 cm) from the edge of the quilt top.

2 Press under ¼" (6 mm) all around the edge of the backing. Pull the folded edge up and over the quilt top so the fold is ¼" (6 mm) onto the top. Topstitch the top and bottom edges first and then the sides.

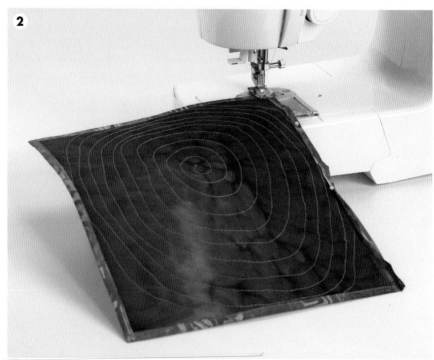

The edges of the quilt can be satin stitched instead of bound, a method that works especially well for fabric postcards and artist trading cards. If the quilting isn't right to the edge, straight stitch ⅛" (3 mm) in from the raw edges. Set the machine for a zigzag stitch that will cover the staystitch. Do not try to make the zigzag cover every bit of the edge the first time around. Do a second pass around the quilt to fill in the satin stitch.

(continued)

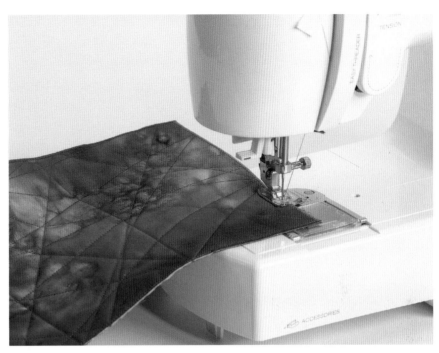

Note: This sample shows another fun way to quilt a small quilt—the pinball technique where the stitch line bounces off the edge in all different directions without cutting the thread.

Another method for finishing the edge of a tiny quilt without binding is painting the raw edges. Straight stitch ⅛" (3 mm) in from the edge of the quilt sandwich and then paint the edges with opaque fabric paint, which seals them and makes them decorative at the same time.

If the gorgeous yarns available tempt you, add one to the edge of your quilt. Straight stitch ⅛" (3 mm) in from the raw edges of the quilt and then zigzag over the yarn laid right at the edge using invisible thread or, if you want it to show, with a thread that contrasts with the yarn.

For a very neat edge on a quilt that has been stitched without the backing on it, follow these steps.

1 Split the backing fabric into two pieces and hem one side of each half. Overlap the hemmed edges and lay the quilt top facedown on the right side of the backing. Stitch all the way around the edges with a ¼" (6 mm) seam allowance.

2 Trim the excess backing fabric and corners. Turn the quilt right side out through the overlap in the backing fabric, poke out the corners with a knitting needle or bone folder, and press. Fuse the overlap shut with a strip of Mistyfuse or add a little more quilting to hold it shut.

A larger quilt that has been quilted with the backing on needs separate binding strips to enclose the edges.

1 Trim the excess batting and backing fabric even with the quilt top. Cut 2"(5.1 cm) wide strips of binding fabric, connect them end to end to make strips that will be long enough for the four sides, and press them in half, wrong sides together. Cut two of the binding strips to the exact length of the top and bottom edges of the quilt. Sew a binding strip to the top edge of the back of the quilt with all raw edges even.

2 Pull the binding around to the front and topstitch the folded edge so it just covers the previous stitching, which should place the topstitching on the reverse at the very edge of the binding on the back. Repeat for the bottom edge of the quilt.

3 Measure the side edges of the quilt and add one inch (2.5 cm) when you cut the binding strips to length. Sew the strips to the back of the quilt, extending the ends ½" (1.3 cm) beyond the top and bottom edges. Fold in the ends, pin, and topstitch the binding, backstitching at the ends.

For a more concealed stitching on the binding, follow these steps.

1 Sew the binding strips to the top of the quilt first.

2 Fold the strip around to back, and pin the folded edge to the back by placing the pins in the seam line on the front. Remove the pins as you get to them, stitching in the seam line where the thread will be hidden.

Display Considerations

Once the quilt is quilted, display becomes the next decision and may affect the binding method you use. Often a simple casing is adequate, into which a wooden lathe is inserted. Sometimes, however, a more professional approach is required, especially if you are selling through a high-end gallery or through an art representative.

Some buyers may require a quick-release hanging system in case the piece is ripped off the wall—the quilts could then be easily reattached to the Velcro-fitted frame on the wall. Other locations require theft-resistant systems. If you are doing commissions, be sure to ask for any requirements necessary for the facility and for the fire marshal before work begins. Some batting is fire resistant and some is not; plus the surface will need to be sprayed with retardant for most public buildings unless the quilt will be displayed behind Plexiglas. Another consideration for hanging commission pieces is the installation logistics—are you willing to climb a ladder and install hardware, or will you require the buyer to handle that.

For most art quilts, a simple casing works well—one that will be hidden from view and will support the quilt for the years it will be hanging on the wall. Cut a 4" (10.2 cm) wide strip of backing fabric or other coordinating fabric that is equal to the width of the quilt (piece it if necessary). Turn under 1" (2.5 cm) at each end of the strip and stitch. Iron the strip in half the long way, wrong sides together. *Before* binding the quilt, pin the strip to the top of the quilt with the raw edges matching the raw edges of the backing, 1" (2.5 cm) in from the side edges. Include the casing in the binding stitching and then hand-stitch the folded edge of the casing to the back of the quilt. Cut a piece of lathe 1" (2.5 cm) narrower than the quilt and drill holes in each end. Insert the lathe into the casing and pound small nails into the wall where the holes are. (For archival quality lathe, paint the wood with latex paint and let it dry for a few days before using.)

Note: For a large quilt or one that will be hung at a show using round "pole and drape," you may need to increase the strip width to 10" (25.4 cm) and leave a little slack in the casing when you stitch the bottom edge down so the pole doesn't bulge out the top edge.

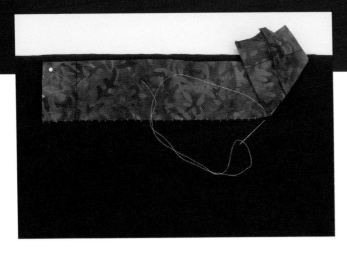

For quilts that have the backing and binding combined, precluding sewing in the casing to the top when a separate binding is added, measure and hem the strip as before but do not iron it in half. Instead, sew a ¼" (6 mm) seam with the *wrong* sides together and press the tube flat with the seam in the center of one side. Hand-stitch the tube down both long edges, with the seam hidden underneath.

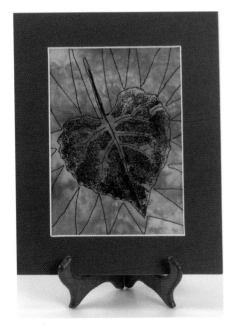

For a rigid but mostly invisible support, make a bound art quilt slightly larger than a pre-stretched canvas from the art supply store. Paint the sides of the canvas a color to match the quilt or the wall if you like. Glue (with archival glue) the quilt or tack it invisibly to the canvas. Add a picture hanger to the back. Leaf print by Wendy Richardson.

A bound quilt can be glued to the top of mat board and displayed or framed with spacers to separate the quilt from the glass. The glass can also be eliminated to better reveal the texture of the quilt.

An unbound quilt can be placed behind a precut mat and glued in place. The matted quilt can then be displayed on an easel, book holder, or plate holder. Leaf print by Diane Swallen.

GALLERY

Provided for your enjoyment and inspiration, the art quilts on the following pages represent a wide range of styles, materials, and themes. Each quilt expresses the vision of its designer; some tell a story while others interpret a common theme in their own special way. You will return to these pages many times, and it's certain you will discover something new every time. Enjoy!

FIBER EDGE CHALLENGE

In the Twin Cities of Minneapolis and St. Paul, Minnesota, the Fiber Edge group of quilt designers proposed a challenge to their members: Take a photo of a gerbera daisy and interpret it in an art quilt. Everyone was given a colored photo and a 24" x 36" (61 x 91.5 cm) black-and-white enlargement. The first location for exhibit was in a wellness clinic connected with a Minneapolis hospital. As you can see, the variety of pieces was extraordinary and ranged from metal to felting to paper. Who says you can't find materials for an art quilt in a hardware store?

This is the photograph and black-and-white enlargement used for inspiration by the quilt designers.

Cindy Trainor works with metal hardware, screen, and pipe to make unusual wall pieces. The combination of metal finishes and textures creates wonderful compositions.

Cyndi Kaye Meier used traditional materials for her interpretation and added a patchwork background.

Doroth Mayer does a lot of cyanotype printing with photographic chemicals and negatives. Her background for this quilt is stunning.

Karen Larsen outdid herself with appliqué, stitch, and texture.

Mary Holland, a marbling artist, painted her background and then added marbled paper petals with a beaded fabric center for her flower.

Nancy Mambi used hand-dyed wool for a background and then felted in the flower.

Rosemary Kessler employed Korean patchwork in silk as a backdrop for a smocked and gathered silk blossom.

Sophie Collier did curved piecing and appliqué and then finished off with beautiful free-motion quilting.

Susan Antell strip-pieced the leaves for her appliquéd version.

Susan Stein put the photo into Photoshop and played with filters to get nine different versions of the original picture and printed them on silk.

Tina Hughes used wonderful painted and dyed fabrics for her lively interpretation.

Wendie Zekowski used papers and sheer fabrics over stitched canvas to build a collage held together with acrylic medium.

QUILTS BY SHARON VITT

"Midnight Garden" is the creation of Sharon Vitt and is made from fused cotton and silk. The use of color and line is outstanding and the quilting masterfully ties the elements of the design together. Go to www.sharonvitt.com to see more of this Ohio artist's exciting work.

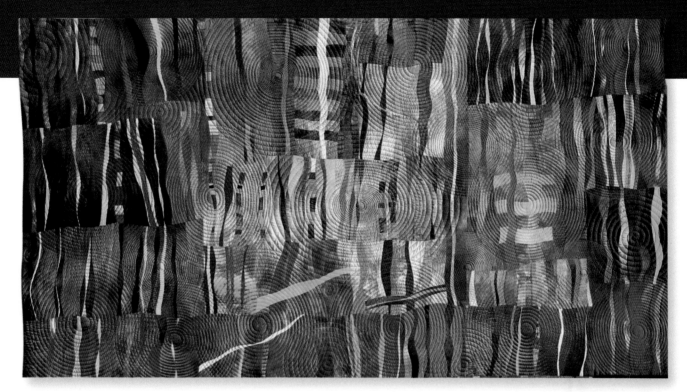

"Pathways" is another example of great use of line, both in the quilt top and in the stitching, plus the use of incredible colors—which makes this Sharon Vitt quilt spellbinding.

"Vertigo" is the name of this Sharon Vitt quilt, which again combines luscious color, line, and stitching.

Blue cyanotype images of tropical subjects contrast beautifully with the rough texture of golden matka silk and other smooth silk fabrics. Simple circular openings with hand-stitched edges frame some of the photos, giving the piece a serene feel. 20½" x 21½" (52 x 54.5 cm)

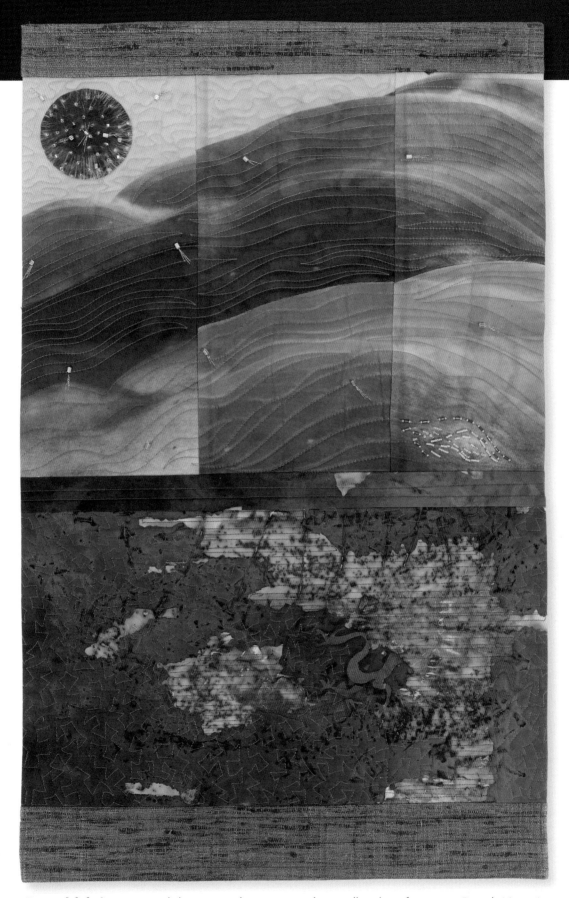

Rusted fabric, a painted dragon, and cyanotype photos all make reference to Doroth Mayer's difficult battle with breast cancer. Beading and stitching enhance the surface and support the powerful elements of the quilt's theme. 20" x 31½" (51 x 80 cm)

Photos and commercial fabrics mix for a wonderful tribute to home and family by Doroth Mayer. Altering of the photos in Photoshop makes them somewhat stylized. Rather than lining up the photos in rows, Doroth has interspersed color and pattern so the viewer is fascinated by the composition, even if they don't know the people featured. 34" x 34" (86.5 x 86.5 cm)

Again Doroth uses very different textures, photo images, rusted fabric, stitching, and embellishment to express the powerful emotions experienced during her battle with breast cancer. 18" x 30" (45.5 x 72 cm)

Another charming tribute to home and family uses cyanotype printing as a backdrop for fun embellishments made with lace and Angelina. Doroth Mayer is a master at integrating various elements that are not at all alike into an artful and nostalgic piece. 24" x 30" (61 x 76 cm)

Doroth Mayer's "Summer Blues" commemorates renegade sunflowers that showed up in her yard. The photographs were manipulated on the computer, turned into negatives, and printed with cyanotype chemicals. The fabrics used with the photo are bits and pieces that also sort of appeared in her stash.

Rosemary Kessler makes wonderful quilts of all kinds. This one features plays on words—the woman in the birdhouse whistles for the black birds that surround her. Words printed onto fabric are combined with commercial fabric, unusual fabrics in the bird house, and very graphic background fabric to make a stunning and whimsical quilt. 19" x 21" (48.5 x 53.5 cm)

Rosemary Kessler collected a year's worth of fabric journal pages featuring her garden into a hanging piece that always attracts an audience. Different surface design techniques and the use of text make each section one to study and enjoy. 26" x 48" (66 x 122 cm)

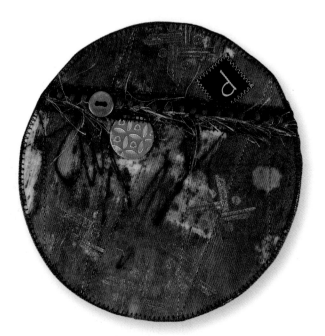

These seven little pieces illustrate what Tina Hughes loves—printing and circles. From potato printing to meat tray printing to printing with disperse dyes to printing with a transparency sheet, color and composition *can* be packed into a 6" (15.2 cm) circle! Notice the different edge finishes—couched yarn, zigzag or herringbone stitch, binding (finished and raw edge), and corded with zigzag.

Simple printing with bubble wrap and a stencil make a complex background for the transfer images, buttons, and tiny squares of fabric on this Tina Hughes quilt. Circles of stitching and a beaded line add motion while a swath of sheer netting lends mystery and texture. Add the complementary color scheme of red and green, and you have a small piece with great impact. 8" x 13½" (20.5 x 34.5 cm)

"Dreaming of a Nest" by Tina Hughes began with photo transfer paper on which a photo was printed. Tina printed circles on the corner and scratched into the polymer coating around the dove before ironing the photo onto fabric. Patchwork with additional printing in monochromatic colors creates borders for the bird. After quilting by hand and machine, she hand-stitched on imported handmade paper squares and tiny sticks. 27" x 20½" (68.5 x 52 cm)

This beautiful quilt was made to commemorate a vacation to Hawaii. Tina Hughes created this piece using visual and actual texture, warm and exciting color schemes, and wonderful hand and machine stitching. The leaves were printed with fabric paint and many of the fabrics were hand-dyed to result in a complex quilt made up of simple elements. 28" x 27" (71 x 68.5 cm)

This wonderful wool quilt started as a thrift store blanket. Acid dyes and Wendie Zekowski's talent for dyeing turned it into spectacular surface for stitching and beading, full of depth and texture. The small blocks are butted and zigzagged together and the outer edge is hand-stitched to the backing with yarn. 24" x 30" (61 x 76 cm)

A friend's pants became the raw material for this Wendie Zekowski quilt. Starting as lime green, the wool fabric was over-dyed in rich and varied colors using acid dye. After piecing the strips together, Wendie spent many hours adding French knots by hand using variegated thread. 24½" x 36½" (62 x 92.5 cm)

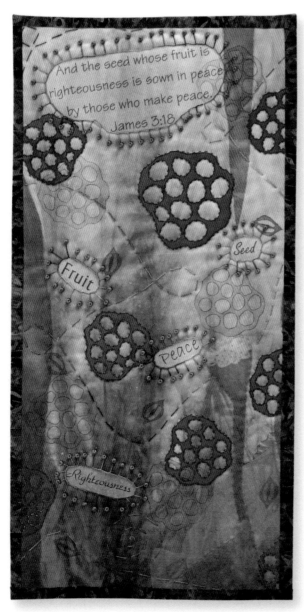

In 2010 Elizabeth Palmer-Spilker and I challenged each other to make a quilt a month for the year and base it on the measurements 20" x 10" (51 x 25.5 cm) with the color wheel as the color focus. Whereas I used the color of the wheel as the whole background, Elizabeth used the color she chose for the month as an accent and experimented with all kinds of printing and surface design techniques. This piece, called "Seeds," is done with photos and words printed on organza, stamped images using handmade stamps, beading, and embroidery.

2010 Challenge Project "Under the Sun." This piece employs gel medium photo transfer, pastel sticks, diluted spray ink, and free-motion quilting.

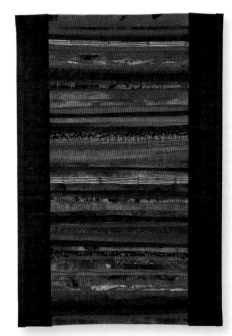

Red Desert. This color study is done with raw-edge strips and machine quilting.

Metro Gardens. Inspired by the Metro Gardens in Columbus, Ohio, this piece shows a photo digitally manipulated and printed. Other techniques include fusing, piecing, hand embroidery, and free-motion quilting.

Sanctuary. This piece was inspired by a cathedral in Paris and is machine appliquéd and quilted. The bottom edge is satin-stitched and the other edges have faced binding.

FABRICS AND QUILTS BY LUCY SENSTAD

Lucy Senstad, of Aunt Annie's Quilts and Silks in Avon, Minnesota, (www.auntanniesquilts.com) is known for her very unusual art quilts, discharged fabrics, and gelatin prints. This pair of gelatin prints shows the result of taking two prints from the same paint and leaf setup.

These gelatin prints capitalize on what some people would consider flaws in the gelatin pad— cracks and bubbles! The results are fantastic, the creation of an artist with an eye for the unique and the ability to produce complex images with a simple process.

Subtle color changes, soft edges, and complex results on gelatin prints are Lucy's trademark. Here two similar shapes are developed into entirely different images—one is abstract with great depth; the other is Lucy's signature image, the guitar. Remember that fine details can be added with a tiny brush after the gelatin print is dry.

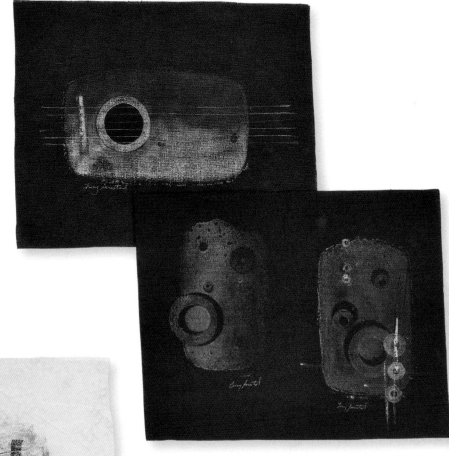

This pair of prints illustrate how simple materials like washers and torn paper, used for gelatin prints, can create complex images by layering several prints over each other.

Two guitars by Lucy, one classic and one modern, show a myriad of tiny details that make them spectacular. Notice the tiny snaps, buttons, and cutout fabric circles that add immeasurably to the overall effect. The classic guitar uses an exotic print beautifully for the face of the instrument, and grid quilting in heavy thread adds texture to the background.

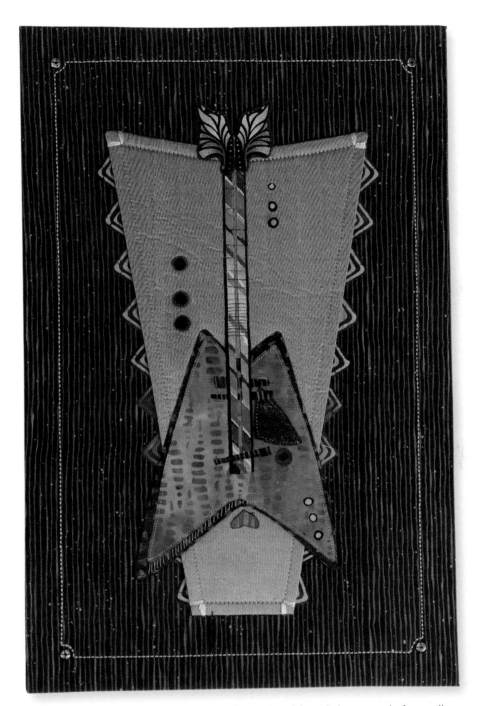

The modern guitar is sewn over a dimensional faced shape made from silk dupioni to set it off. Both pieces have stitching around the edges to act as a frame and are wrapped around heavy interfacing, fused, and covered in the back with a separate piece of fabric to conceal the raw edges of the wrap-around front material.

"Divinations" by Lucy is a masterful mix of ethnic fabrics of all types and a crazy quilt kind of style. Little elements from printed fabrics become eyes and details in the masks, and stitching creates all of the pattern on one. Tabs at the top and beads on the bottom set this quilt apart as unique. It is one you can look at for a long time, constantly finding new surprises.

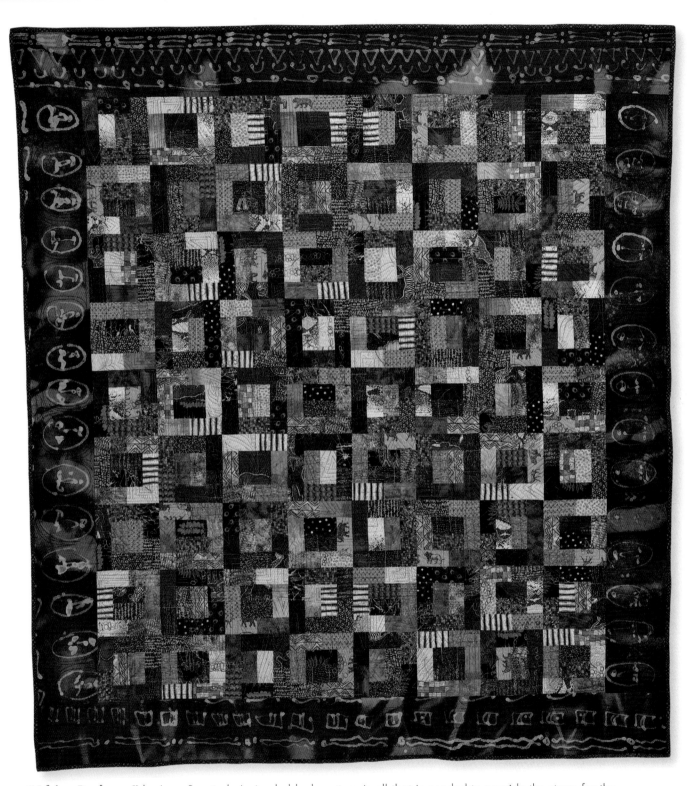

"Africa Beckons" by Lucy Senstad. A simple block pattern is all that is needed to provide the stage for the multitude of interesting fabrics that reflect Africa's images, patterns, and textures. Machine quilting in straight lines, waves, and circles is a subtle but very effective way to add texture and another design element. Discharged masks and other patterns on the border are the perfect finish for a fascinating quilt.

VARIOUS QUILT DESIGNERS

Kit Eastman combines several surface design techniques in her pieces—screen printing, stenciling, Paintstik, and dyeing among others. Her love of nature and the ability to portray it in fabric is complemented by her combination of fabrics, hand and machine stitching, and interesting raw edges. Kit has suspended the piece (not quilted) between two pieces of wood and then added a hanger to the top. 28" x 21" (71 x 53.5 cm)

Sylvia Gleiter of Sun Prairie, Wisconsin, uses the edge qualities and textures in multiple strips of fabric to provide a fascinating backdrop for big hand stitches and beading. The viewer could spend lots of time studying this piece and enjoying its wonderful combinations of color and pattern. The quilt is beautifully framed with matting and glass, another approach to finishing an art quilt for display. 25½" x 14" (65 x 35.5 cm)

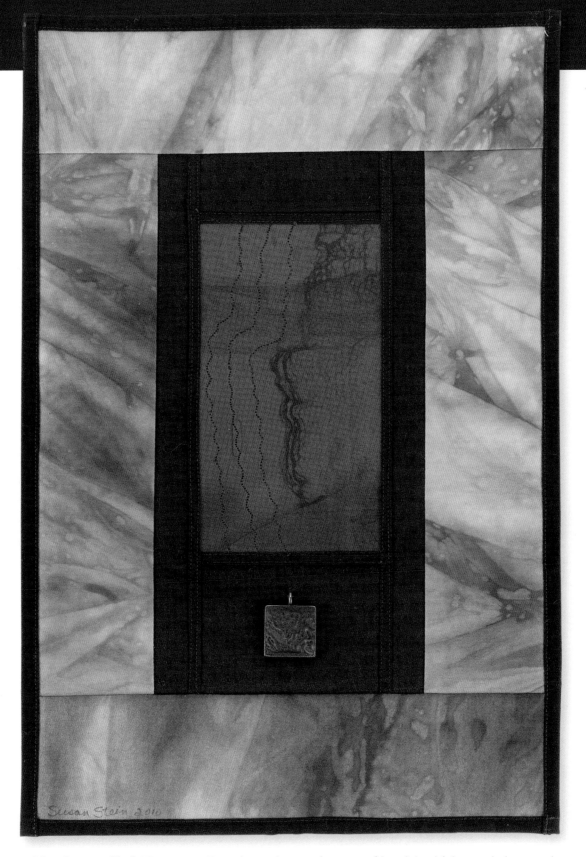

This piece, called "Textures," combines the visual texture of hand-dyed fabric with the actual textures of jacquard woven fabric, copper screen, and embossed polymer clay. Vinegar soaking was used to give the copper its color and pattern. 11" x 16½" (28 x 42 cm)

CROSSING BORDERS RIVER PROJECT

This wonderful exhibit includes the work of sixteen members of the Crossing Borders quilt group in St. Cloud, Minnesota. The group's members regularly challenge themselves to create a piece around a certain theme but most are small individual pieces. "The river CROSSING our BORDERS" project was carefully planned so all the sections would join together to create a continuous representation of the Mississippi River as it impacts each person. The variety of treatments is fascinating—from totally abstract to very realistic—but each section is exactly 18" (45.5 cm) wide. Length was left up to each artist, another feature that makes this series so interesting.

River Road by Chris Hoover.

Nature's Playground by Lavonne Zeman.

A River of Riches by Sarah Howard.

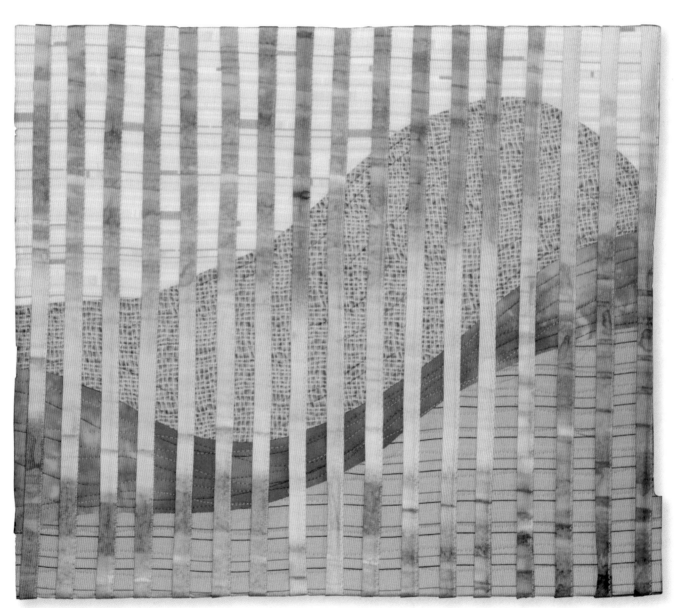

Piece #4 by Sue Beckman.

Piece #5 by Donna Jarve.

THE COMPLETE PHOTO GUIDE TO ART QUILTING

Piece #6 by Deanna Hennen.

A Winter's Night by Beth Probasco.

Skiing by Mary Pat Roberts.

Wild Rose River by Sue Kelly.

Cabin in the Woods by Nancy Kazlauckas.

Aurora River by Jean Imholte.

Floating by Brooke Strassburg.

Little Boy Lake by Jan Steeves.

River Through the Hills by Karen Ferkinhoff.

River Bounty by Donna Kuhl.

The Three Graces by Jane Spolar.

RESOURCES

Angelina shreds and film, stencils, many other things:
www.EmbellishmentVillage.com

Books, impressible foam, art supplies, Lutrador, etc.:
www.MeinkeToy.com
www.joggles.com
www.DickBlick.com
www.quiltingarts.com

Discharge paste, textile medium, textile paints, inkjet
fabric sheets including ExtravOrganza, PearlEx powder:
www.jacquardproducts.com

Gel and acrylic mediums: Golden and Liquitex,
available at art and crafts stores

Hand-dyed fabrics, organza, vintage linens,
and twill tape:
Wendy Richardson, www.QTStudio.com

Hand-dyed fabric bundles:
www.CherrywoodFabrics.com

Paint, photo transfer paper, soy wax flakes,
prepared-for-dyeing fabrics, textile medium, books,
Pebeo Expandable Paint, Jacquard Discharge Paste,
Jones Tones colored puff paint, bleach neutralizer,
dyes and chemicals, info online:
www. DharmaTrading.com

Paintstiks, accessories:
www.cedarcanyontextiles.com

Print paste SH, dye, Synthrapol, soda ash, urea,
Pebeo Setacolor paints and medium:
www.prochemicalanddye.com

Printed images: Dover Publications

Silk roving:
www.TreenwaySilks.com
(now located in the United States)

Stencils, Paintstiks, rubbing/texture mats, foil for fabric,
foil adhesive:
www.LauraMurrayDesigns.com

Thermofax screens:
Nancy Mambi, nancymambi@comcast.net

Threads, Texture Magic shrinking fabric:
www.Superiorthreads.com

Further Reading

Art & Fear, David Bayles and Ted Orland, 1993, Capra Press

Color and Composition for the Creative Quilter, Katie Pasquini Masopust and Brett Barker, 2005, C&T

The Complete Photo Guide to Textile Art, Susan Stein, 2010, Creative Publishing

Design Basics, David A. Lauer, 1979, Holt, Rinehart, and Winston

The Painted Quilt, Linda and Laura Kemshall, 2007, David and Charles

The Quilter's Book of Design, Ann Johnston, 2000, Quilt Digest Press

Screen Printing, Claire Benn and Leslie Morgan, www. Committed to Cloth.com

About the Author

Susan Stein started quilting in 1977 and has delighted in getting other people obsessed with quilting and surface design ever since. A former president and show chairman for Minnesota Quilters, Susan was named Minnesota Quilter of the Year in 2003. She has shared her talents as the author of several books, including *The Complete Fabric Artist's Workshop* and *The Complete Photo Guide to Textile Art,* and has contributed to numerous other publications. As a former quilt shop owner and quilting spokesperson, Susan has taught many classes in Minnesota and around the United States. Many of the hundreds of quilts produced by her hands serve as wall hangings, publication pieces, and store samples, while others are on public display or in personal use.

Dedication

Thank you to all the friends, new and old, who loaned me work. Without all of your wonderful pieces, the impact of this book would have been much diminished.

Index

MORE BOOKS BY SUSAN STEIN!

The Complete Photo Guide to Textile Art

ISBN: 9781589235052

The Complete Fabric Artist's Workshop

ISBN: 9781589236639

The Complete Photo Guide to Cake Decorating
Autumn Carpenter

ISBN: 9781589236691

The Complete Photo Guide to Perfect Fitting
Sarah Veblen

ISBN: 9781589236080

The Complete Photo Guide to Window Treatments, Second Edition
Linda Neubauer

ISBN: 9781589236073

The Complete Photo Guide to Jewelry Making
Tammy Powley

ISBN: 9781589235496

DON'T MISS THE OTHER BOOKS IN THE SERIES!

The Complete Photo Guide to Sewing

ISBN: 9781589234345

The Quilting Bible

ISBN: 9781589235120

The Complete Photo Guide to Felting
Ruth Lane

ISBN: 9781589236981

The Complete Photo Guide to Needlework
Linda Wyszynski

ISBN: 9781589236417

The Complete Photo Guide to Knitting
Margaret Hubert

ISBN: 9781589235243

The Complete Photo Guide to Crochet
Margaret Hubert

ISBN: 9781589234727

The Complete Photo Guide to Creative Painting
Paula Guhin and
Geri Greenman

ISBN: 9781589235403

The Complete Photo Guide to Doll Making
Nancy Hoerner,
Barbara Matthiessen
and Rick Petersen

ISBN: 9781589235045

The Complete Photo Guide to Ribbon Crafts
Elaine Schmidt

ISBN: 9781589234697

ONLINE OR AT YOUR LOCAL CRAFT OR BOOK STORE.

Creative Publishing
international

www.CreativePub.com

OUR BOOKS ARE AVAILABLE AS E-BOOKS, TOO!

Many of our bestselling titles are now available as E-Books.
Visit www.Qbookshop.com to find links to e-vendors!

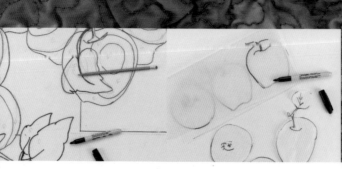

The ULTIMATE reference for all aspects of art quilting—a comprehensive exploration of style options, design elements, and practical techniques for aspiring and experienced quilt artists.

No one can become a quilt artist by simply following instructions. Just as paint artists aren't successful the first time they take brush in hand, becoming a quilt artist takes experimentation and lots of practice. *The Complete Photo Guide to Art Quilting* gives you a solid foundation from which to begin your exploration. The techniques, format options, and design principles taught here will help you develop your skills, while hundreds of art quilts and art cloths designed by others will inspire you to develop your own artistic voice.

Get Started:
* Set up your work space
* Choose formats
* Select fabrics and embellishments
* Audition techniques
* Challenge yourself with new ideas

Build Skills:
* Study design elements
* Practice construction
* Learn fabric manipulation
* Experiment with color
* Diversify your subject matter

If you are just beginning, five easy projects are included to give you a chance to try different methods and formats. An extensive gallery of art quilts by many artists exhibits the vast range of possibilities. Your creative journey into the world of art quilting begins here!

* *

Also Available:

The Complete Fabric Artist's Workshop
978-1-58923-663-9

The Quilting Bible, 3rd Edition
978-1-58923-512-0

The Complete Photo Guide to Textile Art
978-1-58923-505-2

ISBN: 978-1-58923-689-9

Creative Publishing international

EAN
9 781589 236899

52499

www.creativepub.com